I LOVE CORN

LISA SKYE

Foreword by Jean Tang
Photography by Bill Brady

**Andrews McMeel
Publishing, LLC**
Kansas City • Sydney • London

Andrews McMeel Publishing, LLC
an Andrews McMeel Universal company
1130 Walnut Street, Kansas City, Missouri 64106

www.andrewsmcmeel.com

12 13 14 15 16 WKT 10 9 8 7 6 5 4 3 2 1

ISBN: 978-1-4494-1816-8

Library of Congress Control Number: 2011944564

Design: Holly Ogden
Photography: Bill Brady
Food Stylist: Brian Preston-Campbell
Assistant Food Stylist: Laurie Knopp
Photos courtesy of iStockphoto.com: page 53

ATTENTION: SCHOOLS AND BUSINESSES
Andrews McMeel books are available at quantity discounts with bulk purchase
for educational, business, or sales promotional use. For information, please
e-mail the Andrews McMeel Publishing Special Sales Department:
specialsales@amuniversal.com

TO MY FATHER, HANK, MY MOTHER, JOYCE,
AND MY BROTHER, BRIAN.
I AM ETERNALLY GRATEFUL YOU ARE MY FAMILY.
I LOVE YOU.

CONTENTS

FOREWORD

by Jean Tang

This is no ordinary cookbook. It's a labor of love–and not just a love of corn.

Sure, the book is called *I Love Corn*, but it's about more than Lisa Skye's great (and greatly celebrated) love of the star ingredient. It is inspired by her dad, who died tragically on Valentine's Day 2004, and by her mother and brother, who are never far from her side. Lisa has an abiding admiration for the food industry, in which she made her New York City debut, and in which she immediately became a key player in the early 2000s. This book is also proof of her dedication to strangers who, like herself, have lost a parent. A portion of the proceeds from the sale of this book will be donated to The Dougy Center, an organization dedicated to helping grieving children and families. As a result, I will forever pair my personal corn cravings with charitable thoughts. Her remarkable spirit shines through the sunny yellow, cheerful pages filled with a warm-hearted, community-loving collection of recipes.

I met Lisa just two years after her father, Hank, passed away. It was friendship at first sight—and one that rose above food, travel, and other mutual interests into a rare and delicious synergy of personal growth. If there's one thing I know about Lisa, it's that, underneath her bubbly aura, she has a trumping, self-reliant, rock-star integrity. She brings it everywhere: from her career to leadership, hyperactive networking, and, finally, corn cooking.

The recipes have been collected from some of the top chefs across the country, and have been meticulously tested for the home cook. One day in early 2011, I asked Lisa, "What are you doing this weekend?" She responded, "Oh, just testing corn recipes." This went on throughout spring, summer, and well into fall. Her friends and family got in on the action, too. "Didn't so-and-so make that appetizer for you already?" I'd ask. "Yes, but I'm just testing it again to make sure," she'd say. She couldn't (and still can't) seem to get enough of her beloved, buttery-sweet vegetable.

For the reader, this bodes well. Like love itself, *I Love Corn* is full of flavor, texture, and pleasure. Corn that anchors chowder (stewed with clams and bacon) or that lends its grainy texture to muffins may not be new, but as reimagined by Douglas Katz and Jay Foster, it's ceremonious and highly decadent. More unusual is corn in ceviche, corn in wontons, even corn ice cream. Michelle Bernstein's corn isn't simply *in* her ceviche, it forms the key ingredient, swapping out the seafood. A golden corn puree from Peter Eco sweetens ravioli. Jonathon Sawyer pairs bright yellow kernels with crabmeat and gnocchi. Corn quiche? Corn salsa? Northern Thai-style corn fritters? All are here, courtesy of celebrated and private chefs with a shared regard for the main ingredient, and creativity to spare. Here's wishing you all of the joy of an infinite, corn-filled summer!

INTRODUCTION

When I set out in 2007 to gather recipes for *I Love Corn*, it was supposed to be a relatively simple project I would complete as part of a three-month leadership program I was enrolled in through Landmark Education. Although creating an internationally distributed and properly published cookbook was certainly a glimmer of hope in my mind, it was not at all the end goal I had set out to achieve in those three months. At the time, I clearly did not realize the magnitude of what was fully possible.

On Valentine's Day 2004, I lost my father, Henry "Hank" Skokowski. He was six weeks into a two-month, soul-searching dream vacation in New Zealand and Australia, when he was hit and killed by a drunk driver while driving a motorcycle along the Great Ocean Road. On that morning, I felt my world come crumbling down, and that is how I continued to feel for the next six months as I struggled to deal with the loss of my father while simultaneously picking up the pieces of the life he left behind to my brother and me. Fortunately I have amazing friends and a small but loving family who helped me emotionally, physically, and spiritually through this difficult time.

Many people reading this may know what it is like to lose a parent. Happily, others have not experienced this life-altering tragedy. On some level, I feel that all of us—regardless of the circumstances in our own lives—can empathize with the inner earthquake that results from such a loss. Not only do we have to deal with the emotional devastation, but also, amid swimming in a sea of sadness, the details of your parent's life have to be attended to—and those details can be quite overwhelming in the middle of grief.

I have always wanted to give back in some way as a token of appreciation and gratitude to the universe as a result of the incredible support I received during that time in my life. The result of that burning desire is this cookbook. Why call it *I Love Corn,* you ask? Well, for one thing, I do *love* corn! I love it in salads, salsas, and muffins; I own a corn-shaped timer, a wooden corn-shaped serving bowl, corn magnets, and I always have a stockpile of canned corn in my pantry. Corn goes great with everything! Okay, okay. I also chose to write this cookbook because I run in circles with many generous and loving chefs, both professional and lay, and so it felt like a natural way to gather my community to support a worthy cause.

Awhile back, I discovered The Dougy Center (www.dougy.org), an amazing organization that gives much-needed support to children and families grieving the loss of mothers, fathers, or siblings. I am thrilled to know that professional organizations exist solely for the purpose of helping others with what my brother and I dealt with when our dad died. A large portion of the proceeds from the purchase of this book will be donated to The Dougy Center in Portland, Oregon.

If you are reading this now, you may have an active interest in making a difference in the lives of children who have lost a parent, you may be someone who just loves corn—or perhaps you're both, just like me!

From flapjacks to fritters to fancy fresh ice cream, this book is about to blow your mind with the diversity of dishes you'll find possible using our favorite vegetable—corn! The best part is that, if you're like me, you won't be able to decide which one you like the most. In which case, you'll just have to try them all!

Starting with breakfast, you'll be surprised by Peter Giannakas's Corn Flapjacks with Fresh Ricotta, when the crunch of the cornmeal, followed by the swirl of sweet and creamy cheese, tantalizes your taste buds first thing in the morning. Although, maybe you're in the mood for something more savory, and so you whip up a batch of farmerbrown owner Jay Foster's Jalapeño Corn Muffins with a good old-fashioned pat of butter. These moist morsels can also be saved and paired in the afternoon when you're serving Brooklyn-based Guillaume Thivet's Fresh Corn Gazpacho, exploding with such flavors as garlic, jalapeño, fresh basil, and lime. Guillaume says it reminds him of his home in the south of France, which couldn't be farther from the influence of Hong Thaimee's delicious Chiang Mai Sweet Corn Fritters made with coconut and curry. She pairs these tasty treats with a tangy cucumber relish that is, as she says, "so simple to make." I wonder if one batch will be enough!

As the day carries on, you may find you have meat and potatoes on your mind. In that case, Seth Koslow's Sliced Sirloin with Spicy Corn, Shiitake, and Bacon Salsa will delight your dinner guests when the juicy beef goodness melds with the mushrooms and beautiful bacon flavors. Seafood lovers will celebrate when James Beard Award–winning chef Gabriel Rucker pleases your palate with his Roasted Salmon topped with a complex Corn Salad with a kick and fresh green herbs. And I personally rejoice the day Jimmy Bradley came up with his Warm Jersey Corn Salad recipe—I swear, I made it at least five times in the first five weeks I had my hands on it. It's super easy, and a slam dunk of satisfaction every time—for vegetarians, corn lovers, and just about everyone else alike.

Another home-run recipe comes from Martha Stewart, who donated her method for making Caramelized Corn with Shallots—the perfect side dish to bring to a potluck feast along with North Carolina–native Jonathan Bennett's Yankee Corn Bread, which he serves at Moxie, the Restaurant, in Cleveland, Ohio.

Last but definitely not least, this book concludes with the icing on the cake—cornmeal cake, that is. Yes, I'm talking about dessert! Allen Stafford's Fresh Corn Ice Cream is absolutely positively out of this world. It is not at all what you're expecting (whatever that is), and you will want to eat the entire batch. Trust me. Amanda Cohen, who owns Dirt Candy in New York City, rocks your mind with her Popcorn Pudding with Salted Caramel Corn and Butterscotch Sauce. Whoa! Pichet Ong doesn't disappoint with his Corn Crema with Cherries and Bourbon Chantilly . . .

You get the picture! This book makes me love corn even more than I loved it before, which—for those who know me—is unbelievable.

Before you venture into the wide world of corn yumminess ahead of you, I want to thank you for your time, love, and contribution. I believe in my heart that none of us are alone in this thing called life, and I am grateful to have you as a means for continued creation of abundance all around us!

Say it with me, "Mmm . . . CORN!"

From purchasing to storing to preparing to freezing, there's a lot to learn when it comes to making the most of your love affair with this golden veggie. For starters, you should know that *husking* refers to taking the husk off of the corn; whereas *shucking* means you're cutting the actual kernels off the cob.

BUYING CORN

In a perfect world, you will buy and eat your corn the same day it is picked because the fresher the corn, the sweeter it is, and the better it will make your recipes taste. When buying corn, look for ears that feel plump. Peel down a small portion of the husk to confirm the kernels come all the way to the tip, the rows are tightly spaced, and the kernels are milky if squished with your thumb. The silk at the top should be golden brown in color and slightly sticky. The more silk, the better! The husks should be bright green. Make sure the bottom of the ear, where it was detached from the stalk, is not brown. Brown bottoms mean the corn is a few days old. Never buy old corn or corn that has already been husked.

The corn you find in grocery stores and greenmarkets will be offered in three basic varieties—yellow, white, and bicolor—all of which are examples of sweet corn. White corn is typically the sweetest and most delicate, whereas yellow corn is the sturdiest and most hearty. The popular sweet white corn called Silver Queen is sensational in silky soups or sweet desserts, and the denser yellow corn called Jubilee is perfect for salsas, grilling, and canning.

In the winter months, I suggest buying organic frozen corn. Using frozen also saves a *lot* of time trimming the kernels off their cobs. One 10-ounce package of frozen corn is equal to about 1¾ cups of corn. One medium-size ear of corn yields about ¾ cup of kernels. Therefore, one 10-ounce package is equal to about 2⅓ ears of corn.

STORING CORN

Until you're ready to cook your corn, store it in the refrigerator with the husks on in a plastic bag—ideally for no longer than 1 to 2 days. The cold temperature will help to preserve the sweet flavor.

PREPARING CORN

Unless your recipe calls for grilling or roasting corn with the husks on, remove the husks completely. Remove the silks by gently rubbing a damp paper towel from the top to the bottom of each cob. This protects the kernels while removing the silks completely.

CUTTING KERNELS OFF A COB OF FRESH CORN

Cut off the pointed end from the ear of corn so it stands flat. Hold it in a wide bowl with high sides and use a large, sharp chef's knife to cut the kernels away from the cob, from top to bottom, around the whole cob. The bowl will catch the kernels and their liquid.

COOKING FRESH CORN

Although the age-old and popular technique of boiling corn on the cob can yield good results, it does not have to be the only way you eat every ear. Corn tastes fantastic roasted whole, grilled in its husk, and steamed on the stove, too. Depending on the season, you can pick your preference and get to cooking!

Roasting Corn

Preheat your oven to 400ºF. If the corn has already been husked, brush each ear lightly with olive oil, season with salt and pepper, and wrap tightly in aluminum foil. For unhusked corn, open the top of the husk and remove as much of the corn silk as possible, then close the husk back around the kernels as best you can. Proceed with either foil-wrapped or unshucked corn by placing it directly onto the oven rack and roasting for 45 to 60 minutes. It's ready to eat when the kernels are soft but not mushy.

Boiling Corn

If you prefer to boil your ears, fill a large enough pot with water, bring it to a boil, and place the corn in the boiling water. The cooking time depends on your own preference, usually anywhere from 3 to 7 minutes. Overcooking results in tough kernels.

Grilling Corn

For grilled corn with a mild flavor, soak the corn in its husks in water for about 30 minutes prior to grilling. Grill for 8 to 15 minutes, or until it is evenly heated. Husking the corn before grilling it will produce a more intense grilled flavor, and it will only take 5 to 7 minutes to cook.

Steaming Corn

This is the best way to retain the most nutrients while still enjoying the full flavor of your fresh corn. Pour about 2 inches of water into a large pot, or just enough that it doesn't touch the bottom of a steamer rack placed into the pot. Adjust the burner to high heat, cover, and bring the water to a boil. Cut the ears of corn in half and place them in the steamer rack. Re-cover and let steam for 4 minutes, or until the corn appears deep yellow. Remove from the steamer and serve piping hot, preferably with butter.

SERVING CORN

There are many delicious ways to serve corn to your friends and family. Here are some of the things you may like to try on your corn on the cob: bacon bits, hot sauce, butter and cayenne, homemade basil butter, lime juice and sea salt, just salt and pepper, and just butter straight up.

FREEZING CORN

To ensure you're able to enjoy this sunshiny treat all year round, you'll want to freeze it for the winter. Start by husking the corn and removing all the silk. Bring a large pot of water to a boil while preparing an ice bath in the sink or in an extra-large bowl nearby. Boil the cobs for 1 minute and then transfer them to the ice bath immediately. Let them sit in the bath for 5 minutes. Remove from the water and shuck the corn with a shucker or a sharp knife. Place the corn in 2-cup and 6-cup freezer-safe bags so that your measurements are ready when you want to defrost the corn.

BREAKFAST

ROASTED CORN AND GOAT CHEESE QUICHE
WITH BROWN RICE CRUST

CORN FLAPJACKS WITH FRESH RICOTTA CHEESE
AND CHOPPED WALNUTS

SWEET CORN WAFFLES WITH CONCORD GRAPE SYRUP
AND VANILLA ICE CREAM

JALAPEÑO CORN MUFFINS

CHILAQUILES DIVORCIADOS

CORN AND CHERRY TOMATO HASH WITH
POACHED DUCK EGG AND TRUFFLE HOLLANDAISE

ROASTED CORN AND GOAT CHEESE QUICHE WITH BROWN RICE CRUST

Private chef **TAIDED BETANCOURT** New York, NY

SERVES 6

2 cups fresh corn kernels
(about 3 medium-size ears)

¼ cup olive oil

1 teaspoon salt

5 large eggs

2 cups cooked brown rice

1 small red pepper, seeded and
cut into small dice

1 small bunch scallions, white
and green parts, chopped

Pinch of crushed red pepper

1 cup whole milk

Freshly ground black pepper

¼ cup chopped fresh cilantro
(or parsley, if preferred)

4 ounces goat cheese, crumbled

When I am in Amagansett in the summer, I like to take advantage of the delicious, farm-fresh corn at every meal. This flavorful, light quiche is packed with protein and all the flavors of summer. It is a big hit with my more health-conscious clients. I serve it for breakfast or pair it with a green salad for a light summer lunch. It also works great for entertaining. For a brunch party, I'll make it ahead of time, set it aside, and serve it at room temperature. Feel free to substitute low-fat or soy milk.

- Preheat the oven to broil.

- Spread the corn kernels on a baking sheet and drizzle with 2 tablespoons of the olive oil and ¼ teaspoon of the salt. Broil the corn for 5 to 8 minutes, or until browned and toasty. Set aside to cool.

- Lower the oven temperature to 450°F.

- Lightly beat one of the eggs and stir it into the cooked rice. Press the mixture into the bottom of a 9-inch pie pan to make an even crust all along the bottom and sides. Place it in the center of the oven and bake for 10 minutes. Remove from the oven and set aside.

- Lower the oven temperature to 350°F.

- Heat the remaining 2 tablespoons of olive oil in a small pan over medium heat. Sauté the red pepper and scallions with ¼ teaspoon of the salt and the crushed red pepper for 5 to 7 minutes, or until the red pepper has softened but still has a little crunch.

(Continued)

- Whisk together the remaining four eggs with the milk, the remaining ½ teaspoon of salt, and a few grinds of black pepper. Stir in the roasted corn, red pepper, scallions, cilantro, and goat cheese. Pour the mixture into the crust and bake on the center rack for 30 to 35 minutes, until the quiche is set.

- Let cool for about 10 minutes before slicing and serving warm.

CORN FLAPJACKS WITH FRESH
RICOTTA CHEESE AND CHOPPED WALNUTS

Chef–owner **PETER GIANNAKAS | OVELIA PSISTARIA BAR** Astoria, NY

SERVES 4 TO 6

3 cups self-rising white corn flour (see Contributor Note)

½ cup yellow cornmeal

½ cup granulated sugar

Pinch of salt

½ teaspoon baking powder

1 large egg

2 cups whole milk

2 tablespoons unsalted butter, melted

½ teaspoon vanilla extract

1 cup fresh corn kernels

2 tablespoons extra-virgin olive oil (or enough to cover bottom of skillet)

2 cups ricotta cheese

1 cup chopped walnuts

Hot maple syrup, for serving

I am a huge fan of Latin American cuisine, and my recipe for corn flapjacks pays homage to the arepa. I would bring home a pack of ready-made arepas that I would buy from the local bodega and have my mother warm one up in a buttered pan, melt some mild cheese over it, and drench it in maple syrup. One patty was more than enough because they were quite dense and filling. When designing our brunch menu at Ovelia Psistaria Bar, I thought the original arepas literally would not stack up for weekend brunch-goers, so I would go fluffier and sweeter, like a plate of good old pancakes, and balance the texture by topping them with some creamy ricotta cheese. Warm maple syrup and a side of fruit complete this Latin-inspired dish.

- In a large bowl, combine the corn flour, cornmeal, sugar, salt, and baking powder. Stir in the egg, milk, butter, and vanilla until well mixed. Then add the corn kernels and mix well.

- Heat the oil in a medium-size skillet over medium-high heat, pour ¼ cup of batter per pancake, and cook evenly on both sides, about 2 minutes per side.

- To serve, stack three pancakes on a plate, adding 2 to 3 tablespoons of the ricotta and 1 tablespoon of chopped walnuts between each layer. Top with more chopped walnuts and hot maple syrup.

Contributor Note: You may substitute self-rising wheat flour.

Author Note: This recipe is just as delicious without walnuts, if you have an allergy or simply prefer to leave out the nuts. I recommend you use stone-ground cornmeal to give your flapjacks an extra crunch!

SWEET CORN WAFFLES WITH CONCORD GRAPE SYRUP AND VANILLA ICE CREAM

Pastry chef–owner **LEIGH FRIEND | ELSEWHERE** New York, NY

SERVES 6 TO 8

2 cups all-purpose flour

1 tablespoon granulated sugar

2 teaspoons baking powder

1 teaspoon baking soda

½ teaspoon salt

2 cups buttermilk

2 large eggs

1 teaspoon pure vanilla extract

¼ cup (½ stick) unsalted butter, melted

1⅓ cups fresh sweet corn kernels (see Contributor Note)

Vanilla Ice Cream, for serving (recipe follows)

Concord Grape Syrup, for serving (recipe follows)

When I stock up on Concord grapes at Elsewhere, the sweet nostalgic smell of them makes anyone who's passing take a deep breath followed by a smile—ah yes, the joy of seasons in New York! They are a late-summer fruit, so I love to take advantage of their short season and freeze the ripe juice for later. Simple fresh-churned vanilla ice cream is my favorite, but of course the options are endless.

- Combine the flour, sugar, baking powder, baking soda, and salt in a large bowl. Whisk together the buttermilk, eggs, and vanilla in a separate smaller bowl.

- Whisk the wet mixture into the dry mixture and finish with the melted butter. Fold in the corn kernels just before cooking.

- Prepare the waffles according to your waffle iron manufacturer's directions. To serve, top each waffle with a generous scoop of vanilla ice cream and drizzle with warm grape syrup.

Contributor Note: Yellow or white corn is fine. If you can't use fresh, buy frozen instead of canned.

VANILLA ICE CREAM

1¾ cups heavy cream
1 cup whole milk
1 vanilla bean, split, seeds scraped
5 large egg yolks
¾ cup granulated sugar

- Combine the cream, milk, and vanilla bean and seeds in a heavy-bottomed pot and bring to just before a boil over medium heat. When you start to see bubbles forming around the edges, turn off the heat and let steep for 15 minutes.

- Whisk together the yolks and sugar in a medium-size bowl. Slowly pour the cream over the yolks while whisking constantly to make sure the yolks do not cook and form lumps.

- Fill a large bowl halfway with ice and water and set it aside. Return the mixture to the pot over medium-low heat and cook until the mixture coats the back of a spoon, 10 to 12 minutes. Immediately strain the mixture into the bowl over the ice bath. Remove the vanilla bean pod. Chill covered, until cold, about 4 hours.

- Pour the mixture into your ice-cream maker and churn according to the manufacturer's directions.

CONCORD GRAPE SYRUP

5 pounds fresh Concord grapes
2 cups granulated sugar
1 vanilla bean, split, seeds scraped
¼ teaspoon citric acid, or 1½ tablespoons freshly squeezed lemon juice

- Puree the grapes in a blender and strain through a fine-mesh sieve, making sure to get out as much liquid as possible.

- Combine the grape juice and the rest of the syrup ingredients in a medium-size heavy-bottomed pot on medium-low heat. Cook, uncovered, until the mixture reduces in volume to a syrupy consistency, about 30 minutes. You can test this by putting a plate in your freezer for 10 minutes and then putting a bit of syrup on the plate. If it is the right consistency, it will cool instantly. Remove the vanilla bean.

- If not using the syrup right away, it can be stored in a tightly sealed container in the refrigerator for up to 2 weeks.

JALAPEÑO CORN MUFFINS

Chef–owner **JAY FOSTER** | **FARMERBROWN** San Francisco, CA

MAKES 12 MUFFINS

1¼ cups all-purpose flour

⅓ cup cornmeal

⅓ cup granulated sugar

3½ tablespoons corn flour

1⅛ teaspoon salt

2½ teaspoons baking powder

1⅓ cups whole milk

2 large eggs

⅓ cup plus 2 tablespoons vegetable oil

5⅓ tablespoons unsalted butter, melted

5 tablespoons finely diced, seeded jalapeño (about 2 medium-size jalapeños)

It was love at first taste when I discovered these muffins in New Orleans. I decided I had to have them for my own. They are the perfect way to start a southern-inspired meal: sweet, spicy, and savory. To this day, we use them to cast their spell on hapless customers. They can be eaten for breakfast, lunch, and dinner. Smear on a small pat of butter, drizzle them with sweet honey, or just eat them plain.

- Preheat the oven to 350°F. Coat twelve silicone muffin cups (or a twelve-cup muffin pan) with nonstick spray (see Author Note).

- Combine the flour, cornmeal, sugar, corn flour, salt, and baking powder in a large bowl. Whisk together the milk, eggs, and vegetable oil in a separate medium-size bowl. Add the wet ingredients to the dry ingredients and mix well with a soft rubber spatula. Add the butter and jalapeño. Stir until completely incorporated.

- Ladle the batter evenly into the prepared cups. Bake for 26 to 28 minutes on the center rack, until slightly golden on top.

Author Note: Coating your silicone cups or muffin pan with olive oil or butter also works, but it may make the muffins slightly more greasy or messy to the touch.

CHILAQUILES DIVORCIADOS

Executive chef–owner **CRISTINA CASTAÑEDA | CAFÉ FRIDA** New York, NY

SERVES 4

SALSA ROJA

10 medium-size plum tomatoes, halved

3 cloves garlic

½ medium-size white onion, chopped roughly

2 large pieces ancho chile, such as pasilla or any large dried chile, stemmed and seeded

⅓ cup water

3 tablespoons canola oil

1 tablespoon Maggi sauce (see Contributor Note)

Salt

SALSA VERDE

2 pounds tomatillos

1 serrano chile, stemmed and seeded (jalapeño is also okay)

1 clove garlic

¼ medium-size white onion

¾ cup chopped fresh cilantro

Salt

This very common Mexican breakfast dish is normally accompanied by eggs cooked as desired, and refried beans. When you serve green chilaquiles (tomatillo based) and red chilaquiles (tomato based) on the same plate, they are called "divorced." However, people usually specify either red or green. I think it is very important to try them both and serve them separately on each plate. In Guadalajara, we serve the chilaquiles crispy, so it's important to pour the sauce on the crispy tortillas just before serving. In other regions of Mexico, they serve them soft, so they can sit on the sauce for a longer time. The crema mexicana, onion, and sprinkled cheese on top are a must, as are refried beans on the side! If serving these with eggs and refried beans, place them in the center, between the salsas.

- To make the salsa roja, place the tomatoes in a blender with the garlic and onion and lightly pulse. Do not blend too much—the salsa should be chunky! Remove the salsa from the blender and set aside.

- Roast the ancho chiles in a dry skillet over high heat (the skillet should be as hot as possible, to get a charcoal-like flavor—you're basically smoking them, as they are already cooked) until lightly toasted but not too dark, 3 to 4 minutes. Place the chiles and the water in a blender and puree for about 1 minute, until you can't see the skin of the chiles but you can still see some of the black roasted parts.

- In a wide pan, heat the canola oil over medium heat. Add the pureed chiles and tomato blend. Simmer for 25 to 30 minutes, stirring every few minutes. Remove from the heat and add the Maggi sauce and salt to taste.

TORTILLA CHIPS

20 corn tortillas

6 cups canola oil

Salt

GARNISHES

Mexican sour cream (See Author Note)

Grated Cotija cheese (or feta or Pecorino Romano—a dry and salty cheese)

Chopped white onion

Chopped fresh cilantro

- To make the salsa verde, peel and wash the tomatillos. Place the tomatillos, serrano chiles, and garlic cloves in a medium-size or large, wide skillet and roast over medium heat for 8 to 10 minutes. Do not let them get too dark! Set aside to cool for 8 to 10 minutes.

- Place the onion and the roasted-chile mixture in a blender with just enough water for the blender to start to spin (¼ to ½ cup, depending on how much water the tomatillo draws). If the tomatillos don't draw a lot of water, add some; if they draw a lot, don't add much water. One by one, add the tomatillos and then the cilantro. Again, do not blend too much—the salsa should be a little chunky. Add salt to taste.

- To make the tortilla chips, cut each of the tortillas into eight wedges. Pour the oil into a medium-size, deep-sided saucepan. Heat to 375°F, then deep-fry the tortilla wedges sixteen to twenty at a time, to avoid overcrowding, until crispy.

- Remove the chips from the oil with a slotted spoon and place them on a paper towel–lined plate to drain. Blot the excess oil off the chips, if desired. Sprinkle lightly with salt.

- To assemble the chilaquiles, in a large sauté pan, heat 1 cup of the salsa verde, and when hot, add enough chips so that they are just covered in the salsa. Remove quickly, after 5 to 10 seconds, to keep them very crispy.

- Repeat the same steps to coat other chips in the red sauce in another pan. Make roughly an equal amount of red chilaquiles and green chilaquiles.

(Continued)

- On each of your four serving plates, arrange equal
  portions of the red chilaquiles and the green chilaquiles.
  Garnish each plate with 1 to 2 tablespoons of the
  sour cream, a sprinkle of the Cotija cheese, and some
  chopped onion and cilantro. Serve immediately.

Contributor Note: Maggi is a Nestlé brand of seasoning
sauce. It can be found in the ethnic section of most
grocery stores or in Asian markets near the soy sauces.

Author Note: Mexican sour cream is a mixture of heavy
whipping cream and buttermilk, similar to regular sour
cream but slightly richer and thicker. You can find it in
Mexican grocery stores and sometimes in large stores
such as Walmart. Using regular sour cream as a substitute
is okay.

CORN AND CHERRY TOMATO HASH WITH POACHED DUCK EGG AND TRUFFLE HOLLANDAISE

Executive chef–owner **NAOMI POMEROY** | **BEAST** Portland, OR

SERVES 4

4 large egg yolks

2 teaspoons sherry vinegar, plus more if desired

1 tablespoon boiling water

8 tablespoons (1 stick) unsalted butter, melted and cooled to room temperature

½ teaspoon truffle salt, plus more for serving

4 medium-size waxy yellow potatoes, diced

2 small handfuls ¾-inch-diced green beans (about 10 beans)

2 strips uncooked bacon, cut into ½-inch dice

½ yellow onion, cut into small dice

½ tablespoon extra-virgin olive oil

4 ears fresh corn, kernels removed (about 3 cups)

½ pint cherry tomatoes, halved

½ pound cooked lump crabmeat (optional)

4 slices of your favorite bread

1 tablespoon white vinegar

6 to 8 duck eggs (see Contributor Notes)

I make hash every week at Beast, based on whatever I find fresh at the farmers' market. I always use waxy potatoes as the base (large enough to be cut into a nice ¼- to ½-inch dice), and then whatever else is awesome . . . peas, favas, and morels in the spring; corn, cherry tomatoes, crab, and a little bacon in the summer. . . .

I like to serve the hash with a poached egg. It can be a regular farm-fresh chicken egg or a duck egg, which I like because it brings extra richness. I serve it with a rustic piece of very lightly toasted bread to soak up everything, and I always garnish the egg with something, such as a sprinkle of special salt or chiffonade of basil.

- Preheat the oven to 400°F and place a rack near the top.

- Fill the bottom of a double boiler halfway with water and bring it to a light boil over medium heat.

- Whisk the egg yolks with the 2 teaspoons of sherry vinegar and boiling water until they become pale and warm and reach the ribbon stage, which is when they have become the consistency of semithick cream. Pour the mixture into the top of the double boiler and whisk until tripled in volume. Remove the double boiler from the heat but keep the bowl on top while whisking constantly. Slowly, while whisking, pour in the room-temperature melted butter. Remove the bowl after all the melted butter is incorporated. Adjust the seasoning with truffle salt and an extra dash of sherry vinegar, if desired. Set aside.

(Continued)

- Fill a large pot halfway with water, salt it, and bring it to a boil over medium-high heat. Add the potatoes and cook until *just* tender, not falling apart, 3 to 4 minutes. Drain quickly and run them under cold water to stop the cooking process. Set aside.

- Fill a medium-size bowl halfway with ice water and set aside. Fill a medium-size pot halfway with water, salt it well, and bring it to a boil over high heat. Drop the green beans into the water and blanch for 3 minutes, then transfer to the ice bath.

- In your largest oven-safe skillet over medium-high heat, fry the bacon and onion together for 4 to 6 minutes, until the bacon begins to release some of its fat. Lower the heat to medium and add the oil. Stir in the potatoes and cook until they begin to brown, 5 to 6 minutes, shaking the pan or stirring constantly. Add a little salt and pepper. Add the corn and cook briefly. Remove from the heat and add the green beans and tomatoes (don't cook them—just let them get hot). If using the crabmeat, add it to the hash now, too. Set the hash aside.

- Place the bread on a baking sheet and bake until lightly toasted, 6 to 8 minutes. Remove from the oven and set aside. Turn off the oven. Place the hash in the oven to keep it warm.

- Fill a medium-size pot halfway with water, add the white vinegar, and bring it to a boil over medium-high heat. Lower the heat to medium-low to stop the water from boiling. Poach the duck eggs by placing them in individual ramekins and gently dipping them into the water to turn them out. Don't mess with them until you see the egg whites are cooked, 3 to 4 minutes per egg. Remove the eggs with a slotted spoon so they can drain. (Part of the poaching can be done ahead, as well. You can take them out when they are still *very* soft in the yolk and then place them back in the water for a second to rewarm them later.)

- To serve, place some hash on each plate with a piece of toast next to it. Place a poached egg on top and finish with a dollop of truffle hollandaise and a sprinkle of truffle salt.

Contributor Notes: It's good when everything in this dish is of similar "hash" size, thus I recommend keeping everything under ½-inch dice.

Use heirloom tomatoes in place of the cherry tomatoes for a special touch and even more delicious flavor combination!

It is a good idea to poach a few extra duck eggs, just in case one goes sideways on you and decides to break.

SOUPS

SWEET CORN AND CLAM CHOWDER

EARLY CORN SOUP

SWEET CORN SOUP

FRESH CORN GAZPACHO

CHILLED CORN SOUP WITH NUTMEG

SWEET CORN AND CLAM CHOWDER

Executive chef–owner **DOUGLAS KATZ | FIRE FOOD AND DRINK** Cleveland, OH

MAKES 4 QUARTS

2 tablespoons unsalted butter

1 small yellow onion, chopped finely, plus 2 yellow onions, cut into medium dice

1 bay leaf

1 sprig fresh thyme

Salt

1 cup dry white wine

32 cherrystone clams

4 tablespoons olive oil

1 cup medium-diced celery (about 3 ribs)

Cayenne

1 herb sachet (see Contributor Notes)

1 tablespoon all-purpose flour

3 medium-size ears fresh sweet corn, roasted, kernels removed, cobs reserved (2 to 2½ cups)

1½ quarts heavy cream

3 russet potatoes, peeled and cut into medium dice

½ cup bacon lardons, cooked, for serving (See Contributor Notes)

Fresh tarragon, chopped finely, for serving

This signature fall chowder has become very popular at Fire. We serve it with wild Alaskan halibut, Manila clams, and sautéed spinach; it is also delicious with sautéed diver scallops. The result is a rich, thick, and spicy chowder with a great kick!

- In a medium-size stockpot over medium heat, melt the butter and sauté the finely chopped small onion, bay leaf, and thyme. Season with salt, stir, and cook for 5 minutes.

- Add the white wine and clams. Steam until the clams open, 5 to 7 minutes, depending on their size. Drain and reserve the liquid. Clean the clams by squeezing them, and then rough chop the clams. Chill until ready to continue.

- Place the olive oil in a medium-size saucepot over medium heat. When the oil is hot, add the celery and the medium-diced onion. Sweat over medium heat until tender, 6 to 8 minutes. Season with the salt and cayenne to taste. Add the herb sachet. Add the flour and stir to coat the vegetables. Deglaze the pan by adding the reserved clam juice and scraping the bottom of the pan. Cook until reduced by half, 6 to 10 minutes.

- Add the corn, corncobs, reserved clams, and heavy cream, bring to a simmer, and cook until all the vegetables are tender. Remove the corncobs. Taste and season with salt. Remove from the heat and set aside.

- In a separate medium-size pot, parboil the potatoes: Place them in 4 to 6 cups of cold, salted water and bring the water to a boil over high heat. Once the water is boiling, cook for 2 to 3 minutes. Drain and add to the chowder.

(Continued)

- Heat the chowder to a simmer. Serve garnished with the bacon lardons and chopped tarragon.

Contributor Notes: To make the fresh herb sachet, place two fresh or dried bay leaves, ten peppercorns, and two sprigs of fresh thyme in a culinary sachet or piece of cheesecloth and secure it closed with a piece of culinary twine.

A lardon is a thin strip or small cube of pork fat used for flavoring. To make bacon lardons, buy slab bacon or thick bacon, slice into ½-inch strips, and cut into cubes. If it's a thick slice, cut it in half and then into squares. Cook in a small sauté pan over medium heat with a few drops of olive oil until the fat renders off and the bacon is just crisp, 6 to 8 minutes. Remove from the pan and drain the fat on a paper towel–lined plate.

Author Note: The potatoes should be added immediately before serving, just before you reheat the chowder to a simmer. If you are making the chowder ahead, stop before you add the potatoes.

EARLY CORN SOUP

Chef–owner **HUGH ACHESON | FIVE AND TEN** Athens, GA

SERVES 6

2 tablespoons unsalted butter

1 leek, white part only, cleaned and diced finely (about ½ cup)

1 rib celery, minced finely (about ¼ cup)

3 cups fresh corn kernels (from about 4 medium-size ears)

1 medium-size bouquet garni of fresh thyme and fresh or dried bay leaf (See Author Note)

½ vanilla bean, split, seeds scraped

1 cup peeled and cubed russet potato (1-inch cubes)

4 cups water

¼ cup heavy cream

1 cup coconut milk

Salt and freshly ground black pepper

When I was young and spending summers at our cottage an hour north of Toronto, Canada, corn season was a revered stretch of late summer. "Peaches and cream" was what we called the sweet, rich, bicolored corn from the local farms. It required about thirty seconds of cooking and was then slathered with fresh butter and a sprinkling of salt. That was it, for lunch and dinner, most every day. Wonderful.

This recipe encapsulates the same freshness but has exotic overtones from the coconut milk and vanilla. It's a simple soup that works well with lobster, crab, or shrimp, if you want to make it more of a meal.

- Melt the butter in a large soup pot over medium heat. Sauté the leek and celery until soft but not browned, 5 to 7 minutes. Add the corn, bouquet garni, vanilla bean pod and seeds, and potato. Cook for 2 minutes over medium heat. Add the water and cover. Continue cooking over medium heat, not boiling. Cook for 15 minutes. Lower the heat to medium-low and cook for 5 to 10 minutes more, until the potatoes are soft.

- Add the cream and coconut milk and return to medium heat. Continue cooking covered for about 5 minutes. Remove from the heat, remove the bouquet garni and vanilla bean pod, and carefully puree the hot soup in a blender, working in batches. Pass through a fine-mesh strainer.

- Season with salt and pepper to taste and serve.

Author Note: To make your own bouquet garni, simply tie together 3 long sprigs of thyme and 1 bay leaf with string or butcher's twine.

SWEET CORN SOUP

Executive chef and co-owner **DAN BARBER** | **BLUE HILL AT STONE BARNS** Pocantico Hills, NY

SERVES 4

3 tablespoons olive oil

2 medium-size white onions, chopped finely

2 medium-size carrots, chopped finely

4 medium-size shallots, sliced

2 cloves garlic, chopped

15 ears fresh corn, kernels removed (about 11 cups)

2 pieces star anise

10 sprigs fresh thyme, tied in a bunch

5 quarts corn or vegetable stock

Salt and freshly ground black pepper

I think M. F. K. Fisher said the best way to eat fresh corn is to pick it yourself, run from the field as fast as you can, peel it, and throw it into a pot of already-boiling water. That's good advice, although making sweet corn soup is a pretty delicious alternative.

- In a medium-size pot, heat the olive oil over medium heat. Add the onions and carrots, and cook until lightly caramelized, 8 to 10 minutes. Add the shallots and garlic, and cook for 5 more minutes. Add the corn and cook for an additional 8 to 10 minutes, stirring frequently. Add the star anise and thyme, and cook for 2 minutes. Add the stock and simmer for 10 minutes. Season with salt and pepper to taste.

- Remove the star anise and thyme. Working in two batches, pour half of the soup into a blender. Secure the lid by covering it with a towel and holding down while pureeing. Pour the remaining soup into the blender and puree. Strain it through a fine-mesh sieve and serve.

FRESH CORN GAZPACHO

Executive chef **GUILLAUME THIVET** | **CADAQUÉS** Brooklyn, NY

SERVES 4

2 small ears corn, unhusked

1 medium-size tomato, seeded and chopped (preferably Jersey fresh)

3 cups tomato juice

1 large unpeeled cucumber, diced

½ cup finely diced white onion

½ jalapeño, seeded and minced

1 clove garlic, minced

3 tablespoons freshly squeezed lime juice

¼ teaspoon freshly ground black pepper

Salt

2 tablespoons minced fresh basil leaves, for garnish

Summer is my favorite season. I was born in the southwest of France, and we get a lot of influence from Spain, spicewise. I remember eating gazpacho like people eat bread in France. One day I decided to elevate my standards and create this unique gazpacho. Everything about it reminds me of my home. The flavors are unexpected. The jalapeños make it spicy, but the creaminess of the corn gives it a nuttiness, which makes for a fantastic combination. It has an intense flavor from the corn but is still a refreshing, light, summery cold soup. I suggest eating it with a thick slice of grilled country bread rubbed with garlic and brushed with olive oil.

- Preheat the grill to 325°F.

- Grill the ears of corn with the husks on for 10 to 15 minutes, or until the husks are burned, turning every 4 to 5 minutes. Remove the ears from the grill and let them cool.

- Remove and discard the husks and then slice the kernels from the cobs. Measure 1 cup and either discard the rest or set it aside for another use.

- Combine all the ingredients, except the basil, in a large bowl and stir until mixed together. Season with salt to taste. Refrigerate for at least 1 hour before serving.

- To serve, ladle the gazpacho into bowls and garnish with the minced basil leaves.

Author Note: This recipe is great to make a day in advance, so the flavors have more time to meld together.

CHILLED CORN SOUP WITH NUTMEG

Chef–restaurateur **DANIEL BOULUD** | **DANIEL** New York, NY

SERVES 4 TO 6

3 cups chicken stock

8 ears fresh corn, husked, cleaned, kernels removed, cobs reserved (about 6 cups)

1 cup whole milk

1 tablespoon sweet cream butter

½ cup chopped white baby onions (10 to 12 baby onions)

½ teaspoon freshly grated nutmeg, plus more for garnishing

Pinch of granulated sugar (optional)

4 drops Tabasco

Salt and freshly ground black pepper

1 tablespoon minced fresh chives, for garnishing

This is my simple and light take on a classic American corn soup, and is similar to the one I serve at DANIEL in late summer. I add nutmeg to enhance the sweet, mild flavor of the fresh corn, but without overpowering it. You can garnish the soup with a variety of ingredients, such as tomato cut into small dice, thin slices of celery, and cooked lobster or shrimp sliced into thin medallions. You could also serve it warm as corn chowder, adding chopped and cooked vegetables such as carrots, celery, leeks, potatoes, and garlic. The soup can be prepared up to eight hours in advance, and kept covered and refrigerated.

- In a large stockpot over high heat, bring the chicken stock to a boil. Add the corncobs and milk. Simmer for 5 minutes, then discard the cobs and set aside the broth, but keep it warm.

- In a medium-size saucepan over low heat, melt the butter. Add the onions and sweat until very soft, 4 to 5 minutes, stirring often.

- Increase the heat to medium, add the corn kernels and nutmeg, toss well, and sweat for 5 minutes. Add the hot stock mixture, the sugar (if using), and the Tabasco. Add salt and pepper to taste. Bring to a boil and simmer gently for 20 minutes.

- Let cool, then puree in a blender until very smooth. Transfer the soup to a freezer-safe container, season to taste, cover, and chill in the freezer for 90 minutes or in the refrigerator for 3 to 4 hours, stirring occasionally.

- Serve the soup in chilled individual soup bowls, garnished with minced chives and a pinch of grated nutmeg.

STARTERS

LOBSTER AND CORN BRUSCHETTA

GRILLED CORN AND CHICKEN EMPANADAS
WITH CHIPOTLE DIPPING SAUCE

CORN "CEVICHE" IN CORN WATER

ARANCINI DI RISO WITH SWEET CORN AND TRUFFLES

SERENADE VEGETABLE TACOS

CHIANG MAI SWEET CORN FRITTERS
WITH CUCUMBER RELISH

LIQUID "GOLD" CORN RAVIOLI

CHILLED LITTLENECKS ON THE HALF SHELL
WITH CLAM BAKE RELISH

ROASTED CORN WONTONS

LOBSTER AND CORN BRUSCHETTA

Executive chef–owner **DOMINIC GIULIANO** | **CHOZA TAQUERIA** New York, NY

SERVES 4

2 tablespoons extra-virgin olive oil, plus additional for drizzling

2 medium-size ears fresh corn, kernels removed (1½ cups)

1 medium-size red pepper, seeded and diced

2 shallots, minced

1 tablespoon curry powder

⅓ cup heavy cream

2 tablespoons minced cilantro, plus additional leaves for garnish

2 tablespoons minced scallions, white and green parts (about 4 scallions)

1 (1½-pound) lobster, cooked, cleaned, and diced into ¼-inch pieces

Salt and freshly ground black pepper

1 French baguette, cut into ½-inch slices

½ avocado, pitted and sliced very thinly

I love this dish because it brings together some of my favorite flavors of summer, and reminds me of growing up near the ocean in Southern California. It's always a crowd-pleaser at any dinner party. I have found that making a little extra is always important because these little bites are addictive. If you're feeling creative, try replacing the lobster with blue crab or shrimp for a new or different twist on this recipe. And don't forget to serve these colorful bites with a nice glass of chilled rosé.

- Preheat the oven to 400°F.

- Heat the olive oil in a large sauté pan over medium heat. Add the corn, red pepper, and shallots. Cook until tender and the shallots begin to appear translucent, 3 to 4 minutes.

- Whisk together the curry powder and heavy cream in a small bowl, and then add to the corn mixture. Continue to cook until the consistency of the cream has thickened, about 1 minute. Add the cilantro, scallions, and lobster. Season with salt and pepper to taste.

- Lower the heat to low. Allow the mixture to cook for 10 minutes so the flavors have time to come together and the mixture thickens.

- Place the slices of baguette on a baking sheet. Drizzle with olive oil and season with salt and pepper. Bake in the oven until slightly toasted, 5 to 7 minutes.

- To serve, place a spoonful of lobster mixture over each of the toasted baguettes. Garnish with a small slice of avocado and a cilantro leaf.

GRILLED CORN AND CHICKEN EMPANADAS WITH CHIPOTLE DIPPING SAUCE

Owner–chef **MARC MATVAS** | **NOLITA HOUSE** New York, NY

MAKES 10 EMPANADAS

2 large ears fresh corn, unhusked

4 skinless chicken breasts

1 cup shredded smoked Gouda

½ cup diced red pepper

¾ cup plus 2 cups mayonnaise

Salt and freshly ground black pepper

1 (14-ounce) package empanada crusts, 10 large disks

6 cups corn oil

1 chipotle pepper (from can), chopped (see Author Note)

1 teaspoon chipotle sauce (from can)

Comfort food is present in every culture's cuisine, and I love nothing more than these little fried packets of goodness inspired by my Latino friends. Using grilled corn gives texture and a slightly smoky flavor that seals the deal. Prep, fry, eat, repeat . . .

- Preheat the grill to high heat, about 550°F. Grill the corn in their husks until cooked through, 15 to 20 minutes. Remove from the grill and set aside to cool. Place the chicken in a medium-size pot, add water to cover, and bring to a boil over high heat. Adjust the heat to a simmer with just a few bubbles and leave in the pot until cooked through, about 15 minutes, then set aside to cool. Dice the chicken into small cubes and place in a large mixing bowl. Remove the corn kernels from the cobs and add them to the bowl, along with the smoked Gouda, red pepper, ¾ cup of the mayonnaise, and salt and pepper to taste. Mix well.

- Place 1 tablespoon of the mixture into the center of an empanada crust and fold over into a half-moon. Crimp the edges to seal in the mixture. Repeat until all the mixture is used.

- Heat the oil in a deep pan or pot to 350°F.

- Carefully place the empanadas in the oil two to three at a time, depending on the width of your pot. Fry until golden brown, 3 to 5 minutes each, turning once for even cooking. Let each empanada drain on a paper towel.

- To make the dipping sauce, combine the chipotle pepper, chipotle sauce, and the remaining 2 cups of mayonnaise. Mix well and serve with the empanadas.

Author Note: Add another chipotle pepper and a teaspoon of chipotle sauce to the mayo for an extra kick of heat!

CORN "CEVICHE" IN CORN WATER

Chef–partner **MICHELLE BERNSTEIN** | **MICHY'S** Miami, FL

SERVES 6 TO 8

Ceviche is one of my favorite dishes; in fact, I have had ceviches on my menus for more than a decade. I first learned to make them in Peru, and refined them with one of my favorite line cooks, Miguel Puelles, a Peruvian who makes the best ceviches in Miami. In this recipe, I swap out seafood for the delicious sweetness of corn and a few other favorite veggies. It still has that delicious gingery, tart zing of the ceviches I have learned to make and serve. It makes a great starter or pass-around.

2 cups fresh corn kernels, cobs reserved (about 3 medium-size ears)

4 cups vegetable broth

Sea salt and freshly ground black pepper

2 avocados, peeled, pitted, and cut into ¼-inch slices

1 pint grape tomatoes, halved

1 cup quartered radishes

¼ cup shaved red onion

3 tablespoons finely diced red pepper

1 teaspoon minced habanero chile

1 tablespoon peeled and minced fresh ginger

3 tablespoons thinly sliced fresh cilantro leaves

2 tablespoons thinly sliced fresh basil

¼ cup freshly squeezed lime juice

¼ cup freshly squeezed orange juice

Bibb lettuce or red leaf lettuce, for serving

- Place the corncobs in a medium-size pot with the vegetable broth. Bring to a boil over high heat, then lower the heat to a simmer and cook for about 20 minutes. Season with salt and pepper. Place the broth with the cobs still in it in the refrigerator until chilled, then strain through a fine-mesh sieve.

- In a large bowl, combine the corn kernels, avocados, tomatoes, radishes, red onion, red pepper, and habanero. Season with a good amount of salt and a little bit of pepper.

- In a separate bowl, combine the ginger, cilantro, basil, lime juice, and orange juice. Pour the mixture into the large bowl with the vegetables and marinate for at least 30 minutes.

- To serve, pour 2 ounces of the corn broth into a bowl and top with a lettuce leaf. Top the lettuce leaf with some of the ceviche. Serve very cold.

ARANCINI DI RISO WITH
SWEET CORN AND TRUFFLES

Chef–owner **DANTE BOCCUZZI** | **DANTE** Cleveland, OH

MAKES 22 TO 24 BALLS

2 tablespoons olive oil

1 cup Arborio rice

½ cup dry white wine

3 cups chicken stock

½ cup fresh corn kernels
(about 1 small ear)

Salt and freshly ground black
pepper

½ cup plus ¾ cup freshly grated
Parmesan cheese

2 tablespoons truffle butter
(see Contributor Note)

½ cup all-purpose flour

3 large eggs, beaten

1 cup panko bread crumbs

8 cups vegetable oil

Arancini are a crowd-pleaser for any occasion. They are simple to make, can be prepared ahead of time, and kept frozen and then fried at any given moment. I remember eating these at a street fair in Milan before my wedding. One of my fondest memories of the matrimony to this day is the arancini. Second to the bride, of course.

- Heat the olive oil in a medium-size saucepot over medium-high heat. Add the rice and toast, 6 to 8 minutes. Add the white wine and cook until the wine is completely absorbed. Do not remove from the heat.

- Meanwhile, in a separate large saucepot over high heat, bring the chicken stock to a boil. Gradually add the hot stock to the rice in small batches so that it just covers the rice, stirring frequently until each addition is absorbed, 4 to 5 minutes after each addition of stock. Add the corn. Continue to stir over moderate heat. Add more stock as necessary until the rice is fully cooked and the liquid is absorbed, 30 to 35 minutes. The rice should be overcooked so that when it is chilled it holds together.

- Season to taste with salt and pepper. Add the ½ cup of Parmesan cheese and the truffle butter. Mix together and cook for an additional 3 minutes.

- Place the flour, eggs, and panko in three separate, shallow bowls. Pour the rice into a shallow baking dish to cool. When completely cool, scoop into balls using a melon baller with a 1-inch-diameter head. Roll the balls in the flour, then the eggs, followed by the panko.

- In a deep medium-size pot, heat the oil to 350°F on a deep-frying thermometer.

- Fry the arancini, 4 to 6 at a time to avoid overcrowding, until golden brown, about 5 minutes. Remove and drain on a paper towel–lined plate.

- To serve, roll the hot arancini in the remaining ¾ cup of Parmesan cheese.

Contributor Note: Truffle butter can be found in most high-end gourmet stores. You can substitute the same amount of truffle oil or truffle puree.

SERENADE VEGETABLE TACOS

Chef **JAMES LAIRD** | **RESTAURANT SERENADE** Chatham, NJ

SERVES 6

1 (24-count) package (4-inch) wonton wrappers

1 small zucchini, trimmed and halved

1 medium-size red pepper, seeded and quartered

2 small carrots, trimmed and halved

2 tablespoons olive oil

1 teaspoon chopped fresh garlic

½ medium-size onion, diced

½ cup diced green papaya

½ cup fresh corn kernels (about 1 small ear)

2 cups finely chopped green cabbage

Salt and freshly ground black pepper

2 tablespoons chopped fresh cilantro

2 cups cooked pinto beans (or good-quality canned beans), drained and rinsed

1 cup tomato salsa (preferably fresh)

This is one of my favorite ways to prepare tacos for my friends and our patrons at Restaurant Serenade. Because of the quick cooking of the vegetables, it allows for more time on the deck and less time in the kitchen. Adding the cilantro to the warm vegetables off the heat helps create a wonderfully aromatic dish. Use good-quality tomato salsa or make your own by chopping tomatoes, onions, and jalapeño peppers. Season the salsa with salt and pepper and chopped fresh cilantro.

- Preheat the oven to 325°F.

- Place each wonton wrapper over a small, overturned metal bowl to form a cup shape and bake for approximately 5 minutes each, or until crisp. Remove from the oven and set aside to cool until ready for serving.

- Slice the zucchini, red pepper, and carrots into ¼-inch slices on a mandoline or by hand.

- Preheat a wok for 30 seconds, until medium hot. Add the olive oil, garlic, and onion and cook for 1 minute. Add the zucchini, red pepper, carrots, papaya, corn, and cabbage, season with salt and pepper, and cook for 4 minutes or until the onion is slightly tender. Remove the vegetables from the heat. Add the cilantro, toss, and keep warm.

- To assemble, warm the pinto beans and put a small amount in the bottom of each wonton cup. Top with the sautéed vegetables and some salsa, and serve.

Author Note: You can use smaller wonton wrappers to make these as finger foods or passed hors d'oeuvres at a party.

CHIANG MAI SWEET CORN FRITTERS WITH CUCUMBER RELISH

Executive chef–owner **HONG THAIMEE | NGAM** New York, NY

SERVES 4

CUCUMBER RELISH

½ cup white vinegar

½ cup granulated sugar

1 teaspoon salt

1 medium-size unpeeled cucumber, halved and seeded

1 small shallot, sliced thinly

FRITTERS

1 tablespoon red curry paste

2 large eggs plus 1 large egg yolk, lightly beaten together

¼ cup coconut milk

1 cup rice flour (see Contributor Notes)

½ cup shredded unsweetened coconut

½ teaspoon salt

2 teaspoons sugar (preferably unrefined)

2 large ears corn, cooked, kernels removed (1½ to 2 cups)

1 tablespoon finely chopped cilantro

8 cups vegetable oil

Krabong, my favorite snack when I was a little girl, inspired me to write this recipe. It's a dish from my hometown of Chiang Mai, Thailand. Not only is it simple to make, it's also aromatic and full of flavor.

- To make the cucumber relish, combine the vinegar, sugar, and salt in a medium-size saucepan over medium-high heat and cook until the sugar dissolves. Remove from the heat and let cool slightly, about 10 minutes. Mix in the cucumber and shallot. Refrigerate for 25 to 30 minutes, until pickled.

- To make the fritters, in a medium-size bowl, mix the curry paste, eggs, coconut milk, rice flour, coconut, salt, and sugar. Fold in the corn, then the cilantro.

- Heat the vegetable oil to 350°F in a deep fryer or medium-size deep pot. Use a medium-size spoon to scoop 4 to 6 rounded tablespoons of corn batter into the oil at a time to avoid overcrowding. Fry until golden brown, 2 to 4 minutes each, turning frequently to cook evenly. Transfer the fritters onto a paper towel–lined plate to drain. Season with salt.

- Serve hot with the cucumber relish.

Contributor Notes: You can substitute all-purpose wheat flour for the rice flour.

Use crushed peanuts, long red chile, and cilantro to garnish the cucumber relish, if desired.

LIQUID "GOLD" CORN RAVIOLI

Consulting chef **PETER ECO** New York, NY

SERVES 4 TO 6

6 ears fresh corn, husked and cleaned (see Contributor Notes)

¼ cup whole milk

2 tablespoons granulated sugar, plus additional for seasoning

2 tablespoons kosher salt, plus additional for seasoning

4 tablespoons (½ stick) unsalted butter

Freshly ground white pepper

6 gelatin sheets, or 3 (¼-ounce) envelopes powdered unflavored gelatin

1 (24-count) package (4-inch) wonton wrappers, (see Contributor Notes)

2 large egg yolks

These are a play on Chinese soup dumplings I created when I was working with Susan Regis at Upstairs on the Square in Massachusetts. What's great is that you can prepare these ravioli and then keep them in your fridge until you're ready to cook them. Once you have them ready, I recommend grabbing a separate pan and adding a tablespoon of butter, blanched peas, asparagus tips, and a few slices of garlic. Once the butter foams up, add lump crabmeat and a little more butter. Adjust the seasoning to taste and get everything warmed to the same temperature. Put the peas and asparagus in a soup bowl and rest four or five ravioli on top. Garnish with a few shavings of Parmigiano-Reggiano, chervil, and parsley chiffonade, and you have yourself a mini masterpiece of liquid corn love!

- Cut the corn off the cobs and set aside the corn.

- Place the corncobs in a large stockpot and just cover them with water. Add the milk, 2 tablespoons of sugar, and 2 tablespoons of kosher salt and bring the mixture to a low simmer over medium-low heat. Barely simmer for 10 minutes. Discard the cobs but leave the liquid in the pot on the heat.

- Blanch the corn kernels in the liquid for 3 to 4 minutes. Reserve 2 cups of the corn water and discard the rest.

- Melt 2 tablespoons of the unsalted butter in a large sauté pan over medium heat. Add the corn and sweat until soft, 8 to 10 minutes, stirring occasionally. Season to taste with kosher salt, sugar, and a little white pepper.

- Puree the mixture in a blender with the remaining 2 tablespoons of unsalted butter. Thin with the reserved corn water. Pass through a chinois (a very fine conical strainer), then measure 2 cups of this corny gold.

- Soften the gelatin sheets in cold water. Squeeze out the excess water, then dissolve in the warm ravioli base. If using powdered gelatin, add without presoaking and be sure to stir constantly, or the gelatin will form clumps.

- Pour the ravioli base ½ inch deep in a 9 by 9-inch glass baking dish and refrigerate until firm. Once firm, cut it into ½-inch cubes and return the cubes to the refrigerator.

- To make the ravioli, place a corn cube in the middle of a wrapper, brush egg yolk around the edges, fold over, and press gently to seal. Be sure to press out as much air as possible.

- Bring a large pot of salted water to a gentle simmer over medium-low heat. Drop in the ravioli two to three at a time to avoid overcrowding and cook for 1½ to 2 minutes each before transferring gently to serving bowls. Be careful—they are very fragile, but super delicious!

Contributor Notes: Any sweet, young corn will do, but I suggest Silver Queen.

I prefer to use wonton wrappers (available in better supermarkets or Asian grocery stores), but you can make your own pasta and cut it into 3-inch squares instead.

CHILLED LITTLENECKS ON THE HALF SHELL
WITH CLAM BAKE RELISH

Chef **ANDREW BEER** Boston, Massachusetts

SERVES 6

2 medium-size ears fresh corn, husked and cleaned

Salt and freshly ground black pepper

2 to 3 tablespoons extra-virgin olive oil

1 medium-size Yukon Gold potato, peeled, and cut into small dice

1 medium-size onion, cut into small dice

1 linguiça sausage, diced

1 lobster, split, cleaned, grilled, chilled, and chopped

¼ cup finely chopped fresh parsley

¼ cup chopped fresh chives

3 dozen littleneck clams, washed, chilled, and split

The roots of this recipe began with a road trip to Wellfleet, Cape Cod. Pat Woodbury of Woodbury's Clams hosted my wife and me for our first clamming excursion. Excited but exhausted from a (very!) early morning in the water, we brought our buried treasures back to the kitchen and began creating what has become our favorite family recipe. We hope you enjoy it as much as we have! It works very well with both grilled and raw clams, and it's great as a first course or as passed hors d'oeuvres. You can also substitute chorizo for the linguiça sausage.

- Preheat the grill to high or 500°F. Season the corn with salt, pepper, and some olive oil. Grill until the corn becomes caramelized, about 5 minutes, turning frequently so that it cooks evenly.

- Fill a large bowl halfway with ice and water and set it aside. Blanch the diced potato in boiling water until tender, about 2 minutes. Strain the potato and place it in the ice bath. Set aside.

- Heat 1 to 2 tablespoons of oil in a medium-size sauté pan over medium-high heat. Add the onion and sausage and cook until the onion is translucent. Remove from the heat.

- In a large bowl, combine the sausage mixture, diced potato, and cooked lobster.

- Using a very sharp knife, stand the corn upright and shave the kernels off the cob and into a bowl. Add them to the sausage mixture, along with the parsley and chives. Season with salt and pepper to taste. Add olive oil as desired.

- Open the clams, top them with relish (either hot or cold), and serve immediately.

(Continued)

Author Note: This corn relish is also delicious on its own. Serve it with iceberg or romaine lettuce leaves to make lettuce wraps, or add it to scrambled eggs for a terrific morning treat.

ROASTED CORN WONTONS

Private chef **J. TYLER BENTINE** Hyde Park, NY

MAKES 36 WONTONS

5 ears fresh corn (or 4, if large), unhusked

2 tablespoons canola oil, plus more for frying

1 small red onion, minced

½ jalapeño, seeded and minced

1½ tablespoons dried epazote (see Contributor Notes)

¾ cup grated Cotija cheese

½ cup mayonnaise

¼ cup sour cream

1 teaspoon cayenne

¾ teaspoon freshly ground black pepper, plus more to taste

Kosher salt

Juice of 1 large lime

1 large egg

36 wonton wrappers

One of my favorite foods in Mexico is elote, or Mexican street corn. This recipe takes the flavors of this great street food, deepens the flavor profile, and is made into an easy-to-handle appetizer. The wontons can be prepared ahead of time and stored in the fridge until ready to be fried and served.

- Preheat the oven to 350°F.

- Soak the corn in room-temperature water for a minute or two. Place the unhusked ears on a dry sheet pan and roast in the oven until the corn is tender and the husk is lightly browned, 20 to 30 minutes, depending on the size of the corn. Remove from the oven and set aside to cool.

- Meanwhile, heat the 2 tablespoons of canola oil in a small sauté pan over medium heat. Add the onion, jalapeño, and a pinch of salt and cook until the onion is soft and translucent, 4 to 5 minutes. Remove from the heat and set aside to cool.

- Remove the corn from the oven, remove the husks, and wipe the corn clean with a paper towel to remove the silk. When cool enough to handle, slice off the kernels and place them in a large bowl. You should have about 3 cups.

- In a large bowl, combine the cooled onion mixture, corn kernels, epazote, Cotija, mayonnaise, sour cream, cayenne, and black pepper. Season with the kosher salt, pepper, and lime juice as desired. The mixture should be fairly loose.

- Heat approximately 2 inches of canola oil in a deep pot over medium to medium-high heat until it reaches 350°F on a deep-frying thermometer.

(Continued)

- While the oil is heating, beat the egg in a small bowl. Working in batches of six, place a heaping tablespoon of the mixture into the middle of each wonton wrapper. Brush the edges with the egg mixture, fold over, and seal the edges by pressing together.

- When the oil reaches 350°F, lower the heat to medium or medium-low and adjust the heat as needed to maintain the 350°F temperature. Fry the wontons until golden brown, and then remove to drain on a paper towel. Serve hot.

Contributor Notes: Epazote, or dried wormseed leaves, and Cotija cheese can be found in Latin markets or the Latin section of your grocery store. If you have trouble finding them, you may substitute dried Mexican oregano and Parmesan cheese, respectively.

If preparing wontons ahead of time, sprinkle them with cornstarch to prevent sticking. Cover tightly with plastic wrap and store in the refrigerator for up to 24 hours.

MAINS

GRILLED NEW ZEALAND VENISON WITH CORN,
COCOA, AND CHIPOTLE RELISH

WARM JERSEY CORN SALAD

ROASTED DUCKLING WITH MUSTARD GREENS
AND SWEET CORN PUDDING

SLICED SIRLOIN WITH SPICY CORN, SHIITAKE, AND BACON SALSA

CHICKEN JAMBONETTE WITH ROASTED FENNEL AND SWEET CORN

FRESH CRAB AND CORN PARISIAN GNOCCHI WITH PANCETTA

GRILLED LOBSTER TAILS WITH SWEET CORN,
CHERRY TOMATOES, AND BASIL

CORN-POACHED HALIBUT WITH TOMATO
AND CHARRED JALAPEÑO CHUTNEY

WARM POLENTA STEW

ROASTED SALMON WITH CORN SALAD AND SALSA VERDE

PAN-SEARED BRANZINO WITH CORN CHORIZO PUDDING
AND SMOKED TOMATO VINAIGRETTE

GRILLED NEW ZEALAND VENISON
WITH CORN, COCOA, AND CHIPOTLE RELISH

Executive chef **BRAD FARMERIE** | **PUBLIC** New York, NY

SERVES 6

CORN, COCOA, AND CHIPOTLE RELISH

4 ears fresh corn, husked and cleaned

Extra-virgin olive oil, for grilling corn, plus ¼ cup

1 small red onion, sliced (about 1 cup)

3 cloves garlic, chopped

1½ teaspoons peeled and minced fresh ginger

2½ teaspoons Maldon salt

1 teaspoon smoked paprika

¾ teaspoon unsweetened cocoa powder

½ teaspoon chopped chipotle

¼ cup sherry vinegar

1 tablespoon fresh cilantro, cut in chiffonade, plus a few whole leaves for garnish

NEW ZEALAND VENISON

1 (8-rib) rack of New Zealand venison with the 2 smallest ribs removed

Maldon salt (see Contributor Notes)

Freshly ground black pepper

The first time I tried New Zealand venison was at the start of my career, when I was cooking in London. From the moment its punchy flavor and incredibly delicious texture hit my palate, I knew it was a rock-star red meat. This dish in particular is a simple, healthy, and delicious celebration of summer, with its bright colors and vibrant flavors. The sweetness of fresh corn mixed with smoky paprika, spicy chipotle, and earthy cocoa offers the perfect foil for the lean richness of New Zealand venison. Both the exotic meat and the unique relish turn an everyday backyard barbecue into a special occasion. Any leftover relish should be used up in a few days, and it is a good topping for anything from ham and cheese sandwiches to shrimp tacos.

- Preheat the grill to high.

- Brush each ear of corn with a small amount of olive oil and grill until lightly charred. Remove the corn from the grill and allow it to cool. When cool, stand the cobs in a large mixing bowl, slice off the kernels, and set aside. (Alternatively, remove the kernels from the cob and cook in a preheated pan until they are lightly blackened and then transfer them to a mixing bowl.) You will also need to grill the venison, so you may want to leave the grill hot.

- In a sauté pan over medium heat, combine the onion, garlic, ginger, salt, and the ¼ cup of oil. Stir every few minutes, until the mixture starts to caramelize and turn golden brown, 6 to 8 minutes. Add the smoked paprika, cocoa powder, and chipotle. Cook for an additional 2 minutes. Add the sherry vinegar and cook until it has evaporated to almost dry.

(Continued)

- Remove the mixture from the heat, add it to the roasted corn, and mix until incorporated. Set aside to cool. Do not add the cilantro yet. The acid of the vinegar will cause it to go brown if added too early.

- Generously salt the venison and season with freshly ground black pepper. Place the venison on the grill and char the meat, turning occasionally to cook it evenly. Remove the meat when it is rare to medium rare, 130° to 140°F on a meat thermometer. Do not overcook the meat as it has little fat and will dry out if not tended to in time. Place the rack on a plate or cooling rack to rest for 8 to 10 minutes. This is a necessary step that will allow the juice to reabsorb into the meat fibers, keeping it in the meat instead of pouring out onto your plate when cut.

- When ready to serve, make a cut between each bone to create six equal-size pieces, each with one bone connected to it. Place a hot grilled venison rib chop on each plate. Add the cilantro to the corn relish and stir, then place a healthy dollop on each plate and garnish with fresh cilantro.

Contributor Notes: You can substitute any fine sea salt for the Maldon salt.

When the mix has completely cooled you can refrigerate it, but make sure that it is brought back to room temperature before serving or the flavors will taste slightly muted.

This is what I recommend you use as a temperature guide: rare, 130 to 135°F; medium-rare, 135 to 140°F; and medium, 140 to 145°F. More than 145°F is not recommended.

WARM JERSEY CORN SALAD

Restaurateur–chef **JIMMY BRADLEY** | **THE RED CAT** New York, NY

SERVES 6

Salt

6 small Yukon Gold potatoes, diced (about 5 cups) (see Contributor Note)

1 pound thin asparagus, trimmed, cut crosswise into 1½-inch pieces

6 medium-size ears fresh Jersey corn (or any sweet corn), kernels removed (4½ to 5 cups)

5 ripe plum tomatoes, seeded and diced

1 tablespoon chopped fresh thyme

¼ cup plus 2 tablespoons extra-virgin olive oil

Freshly ground black pepper

This is one of those come-home-from-work, make-dinner-fast dishes. My longtime publicist and pal, Phil Baltz, and I made this up when we were on the road together, sharing a condo in Colorado. He returned from trout fishing, and we happened to have some corn in the kitchen. We made this dish to see if we could pull off a little challenge we set for ourselves: to make a salad with no added acid—sure, there's a touch in the tomato, but no vinegar at all. As a result, the dish lets you focus on each and every ingredient with no distraction, kind of like making a vegetable side dish into a course of its own. The beauty of it is that the fruitiness of the extra-virgin olive oil really shines.

- Fill a large pot halfway with cold water. Season with salt and bring to a boil. Add the potatoes and boil until tender to a knifepoint, about 5 minutes. Drain through a fine-mesh strainer set over another pot. Transfer the potatoes to a large mixing bowl and set aside. Bring the water back to a boil over high heat. Add the asparagus and boil until al dente, approximately 2 minutes. Drain and add to the bowl with the potatoes.

- Heat a wide, deep-sided, heavy-bottomed sauté pan over medium-high heat. Add the corn in batches, to avoid crowding, and toast until lightly browned, about 3 minutes. As each batch is done, add it to the bowl with the potatoes and asparagus. Add the tomatoes, thyme, and oil, and season with salt and pepper. Toss, divide among individual plates, and serve warm.

Contributor Note: Red Bliss or fingerling potatoes can be used in place of the Yukon Gold.

ROASTED DUCKLING WITH MUSTARD GREENS AND SWEET CORN PUDDING

Executive chef–owner **HAROLD DIETERLE | PERILLA** New York, NY

SERVES 4

4 Muscovy duck breasts (see Contributor Notes)

Salt and freshly ground black pepper

8 medium-size ears fresh corn, kernels removed (about 6 cups)

5 tablespoons unsalted butter

Freshly ground white pepper

2 pounds baby mustard greens (see Contributor Notes)

2 shallots, sliced thinly (on a mandoline if possible)

4 cloves garlic, sliced thinly (on a mandoline if possible)

Every year at springtime, I start looking forward to putting on Perilla's menu something with corn—one of my favorite summer treats! This combination of the creamy corn pudding, bitter garlicky greens, and juicy duck breast is just heavenly! If you find the greens are too pungent for your taste, you can tame them by blanching them in salted water before you sauté them with the garlic and shallots.

- Preheat the oven to 400°F.

- Season the duck breasts with salt and black pepper. Place the duck breasts in a sauté pan over medium heat and slowly render until the skin is crispy. Then place them in the oven to cook for 8 minutes to medium rare, or until the meat reads 130°F on a meat thermometer. Remove from the oven and let the breasts rest for 5 minutes.

- Place the corn in a juicer (or a blender with enough water to juice the corn). Juice or blend very well, until you have about 4 cups of liquid corn. Place the corn in a saucepot and cook over medium heat for 5 minutes, stirring frequently. Add 3 tablespoons of the butter and season quite generously with salt and the white pepper to taste. Lower the heat to low and cook for an additional 10 minutes, or until thick, stirring frequently so the corn does not burn around the edges of the pot.

- Soak the mustard greens in cold water for 5 minutes.

- Heat the remaining 2 tablespoons of butter in a wide sauté pan over medium-high heat. Swirl the pan until the butter begins to brown and bubble, about 2 minutes. Lower the heat to medium-low. Add the shallots and garlic, and sweat for 3 to 5 minutes, until the shallots become translucent. Add the mustard greens and season to taste with salt and black pepper. Cook until the greens are tender to the tooth, 2 to 3 minutes.

- To serve, reheat the duck, then slice each breast into six equal slices and place some slices on each plate. Place a healthy amount of mustard greens on each plate next to the duck. Finish the dish by spooning the buttery sweet corn pudding in the nook between the duck and the greens.

Contributor Notes: You can substitute escarole, kale, Swiss chard, or spinach for the mustard greens.

If Muscovy duck breasts are not available, substitute Peking or mallard duck breasts.

SLICED SIRLOIN WITH
SPICY CORN, SHIITAKE, AND BACON SALSA

Private chef **SETH KOSLOW** Long Island, New York

SERVES 4

3 slices uncooked thick-cut bacon, chopped

1½ tablespoons extra-virgin olive oil

4 ears fresh corn, husked, cleaned, kernels removed (about 3 cups)

¼ teaspoon salt, plus additional for seasoning

Freshly cracked black pepper

2 pounds tri-tip, top sirloin, or flank steak

1 large clove garlic, diced

1 small jalapeño, diced, with seeds (see Author Note)

½ red bell pepper, seeded and chopped

¼ cup beef stock

8 shiitake mushroom caps, cleaned and sliced

I love grilling, which is why I started a backyard barbecue company. To make an ordinary steak pop, I use three of my favorite ingredients—corn, bacon, and jalapeños! Make sure to prep all your ingredients before you begin cooking. Having everything ready will allow for a smooth transition from pan to plate. Also, be patient when rendering the bacon fat. Cooking it fast will limit the bacon flavor in the salsa, and, honestly, who wants to do that?

- Place the chopped bacon in a large pan over medium-low heat and cook slowly until crispy and most of the fat has rendered off, stirring occasionally to ensure that all sides of the bacon pieces cook, 14 to 18 minutes. Once the bacon is crispy, remove it from the pan with a slotted spoon and set it aside on a paper towel–lined plate. Turn off the heat and leave the rendered fat in the pan.

- Place the olive oil in a separate wide, nonstick pan over medium heat. When the oil is hot (but not smoking), add the corn, ¼ teaspoon of the salt, and several grinds of freshly cracked black pepper. Stir the corn regularly until some of the kernels start to darken, 12 to 15 minutes.

- While the corn is cooking, season both sides of the steak with salt and pepper. Grill or broil to desired temperature, though medium rare is recommended (see Contributor Notes). Let the steak rest for several minutes after it is cooked to redistribute the juices.

- While the corn and steak are cooking, place the pan with the bacon fat over medium heat. Add the garlic and sauté for 1 minute. Add the diced jalapeño and red bell pepper and sauté for 1 minute. Add the beef stock. Using a wooden spoon, scrape the brown bits off the bottom of the pan and allow the stock to come to a boil. Add the mushrooms, a pinch of salt, and several grinds of freshly cracked black pepper. Stir to combine.

- Allow the mushroom mixture to cook for 2 minutes, and then add the corn and stir. Lower the heat to low and add the reserved bacon pieces. Allow the mixture to cook for an additional 2 to 3 minutes, stirring occasionally, until the bacon is warm. Season with salt and pepper to taste.

- Slice half of the steak against the grain into approximately ½-inch slices. Arrange the steak slices and remaining steak on a serving dish and spoon the corn mixture over the slices of steak.

Contributor Notes: To grill the steak medium rare, heat the grill to medium-high heat. Season both sides of the steak liberally with kosher salt and freshly cracked black pepper. Place the meat on the grill. Do not flip the steak until the juices start to run off the top (the length of time will depend on the thickness of the steak). Flip the steak once. Remove the steak from the grill when the meat has reached an internal temperature of 130°F. Allow the meat to rest, covered, for 10 to 15 minutes before slicing.

If cooking the steak in an oven, place an empty broiler pan under the broiler. Set the oven to broil (high heat) and preheat for 10 minutes. Season the room-temperature meat with salt and pepper on both sides, as desired. Sear each side of the steak in a stovetop skillet for 1 to 2 minutes per side to seal in the juices. Place the steak in the broiler pan and place the pan 3 inches below the broiler flame. Cook the steak for 5 to 6 minutes or until the internal temperature of the steak reaches 130°F for medium rare. Remove the meat and let it rest, covered, for 10 to 15 minutes before slicing.

Author Note: Use half the jalapeño seeds or no seeds, if you prefer less spicy.

CHICKEN JAMBONETTE
WITH ROASTED FENNEL AND SWEET CORN

Chef de cuisine **SANDRO ROMANO** | **THE MODERN** New York, NY

SERVES 4

CHICKEN

4 boneless chicken breasts (or thighs, pounded thin), skin on

Salt and freshly ground black pepper

VEGETABLES

2 medium-size fennel bulbs, fronds removed and set aside for garnish

2 tablespoons extra-virgin olive oil

Salt and freshly ground black pepper

16 cherry tomatoes, halved

4 tablespoons (½ stick) unsalted butter

2 cups fresh corn kernels (about 3 medium-size ears)

8 garlic cloves, sliced thinly on a mandoline

⅔ cup chicken stock

8 leaves fresh basil, cut into chiffonade

¼ cup Beluga (black) or French green lentils (not the more common brown lentils), cooked

¼ teaspoon freshly squeezed lemon juice

2 pinches of cayenne

2 tablespoons grapeseed oil

When I developed this technique for preparing the chicken, I wanted it to have a ham texture and look, by slow poaching the rolled breast and then slowly crisping the skin in a pan. This way I could name the dish jambonette, which means "ham" in French!

Chicken is an affordable item year-round, and buying the best chicken available is always worth it! Look for organic or free-range chicken at your local greenmarket or in your neighborhood grocery store, and don't forget to pat the skin dry before roasting it!

- Season the chicken breasts with the salt and pepper. Roll each breast into a cylinder so that the skin is wrapped tightly around the outside of the roll. Place on a piece of plastic wrap and roll tightly. Tie a piece of string tightly around the cylinder. It's best to let the chicken breasts rest overnight while tightly wrapped in plastic. If preparing them for the same day, let it rest for at least 4 hours to ensure the proper shape.

- Preheat the oven to 400°F and place a rack in the middle.

- Heat a large stockpot filled halfway with water and heat to 170°F.

- Place the breasts in the pot to begin poaching. After 40 to 45 minutes, poke a hole through the plastic and use a meat thermometer to check the temperature inside the breasts. When they reach 155°F inside, remove the breasts from the water and let them rest for a minute outside of the bath, then remove the plastic. Pat the skin dry.

- While the chicken is poaching, prepare the vegetables. Start by placing the fennel bulbs on their flat bottoms, top side up, then cut in half. Place the fennel halves cut side down, then cut each half perpendicular to the fibers into ¼-inch-thick slices.

- Blanch the fennel by placing it into a small pot of boiling water and cooking for 3 minutes. Drain the fennel in a colander and rinse with very cold water to stop the cooking.

- In a medium-size bowl, toss the fennel with the oil until the fennel slices are coated. Spread out the fennel evenly on a baking sheet. Season lightly with salt and pepper. Place on a sheet on the middle rack and roast for 20 minutes. Remove the sheet, turn the fennel, then roast for another 15 to 20 minutes, or until the fennel begins to brown at the edges. Remove from the oven and set aside.

- Fill a large bowl halfway with ice and water and set it aside. Bring a small pot of water to a boil. Place the tomatoes in the water for 30 seconds. Use a slotted spoon to remove them from the water and place them in the ice bath for 30 seconds. Peel the skins from the tomatoes and set them aside.

- In a wide sauté pan over medium-high heat, heat the butter until sizzling. Add the corn and sauté for 1 minute. Add the sliced garlic and split cherry tomatoes. Toss well and continue to heat over medium-high heat, 4 to 5 minutes. Add the chicken stock, basil, lentils, lemon juice, and fennel and continue to cook for 1 to 2 minutes. Add salt and pepper to taste and add the cayenne for a spicy kick.

- Place the grapeseed oil in a large nonstick pan over medium-high heat. Roast the chicken until the skin gets crisp and light brown, 8 to 10 minutes, turning regularly and using a cover to avoid splattering oil. Transfer the chicken to a paper towel–lined plate to drain.

- To serve, place some vegetables on each plate. Use a serrated knife to slice the chicken breasts thinly and place the slices on top of the vegetables. Garnish with the fennel fronds.

FRESH CRAB AND CORN PARISIAN GNOCCHI WITH PANCETTA

Executive chef–owner **JONATHON SAWYER | THE GREENHOUSE TAVERN** Cleveland, OH

SERVES 4

4 ears fresh corn, husked, cleaned, kernels removed, cobs reserved (about 3 cups)

4 cups vegetable stock (or enough to cover the corncobs)

1 tablespoon unsalted butter

1 cup diced pancetta

1 fresh bay leaf

Parisian Gnocchi (recipe follows; see Contributor Notes)

1 teaspoon minced roasted Fresno chiles (see Contributor Notes)

¾ cup chopped fresh picked Dungeness crabmeat

Freshly ground black pepper

Fresh parsley, for garnish (optional)

At the Greenhouse Tavern we believe that the proximity of the farm and soil to a restaurant correlates to the quality of its food. Cooking with local ingredients is essential, and Ohio corn is one of our favorites. One of our finest summer pastas at the Greenhouse Tavern is featured here. Contrasting with the spiciness of the black pepper, this dish really showcases the sweetness of fresh Ohio corn.

- Place the corncobs in a medium-size stockpot and fill the pot with the vegetable stock until just covered. Bring to a boil over medium-high heat, and then shut off the heat and let the cobs steep for 10 minutes. Strain the stock into a separate container, reserve 1 cup, and save the rest for another use. Discard the cobs.

- Place the butter and pancetta in a wide, nonstick pan over medium-high heat. Render the fat from the meat and heat until the butter begins to brown, 4 to 5 minutes.

- Add the bay leaf and gnocchi to the pan and cook until the gnocchi begin to brown on one side. Add the corn, Fresno chiles, and the 1 cup of reserved vegetable stock. Toss and cook for 2 to 3 additional minutes, or until the pasta and the sauce homogenize. Add the crab and season with freshly ground pepper to taste. Toss again, and add parsley as desired. Serve hot.

Contributor Notes: You can substitute 1 (16-ounce) box of store-bought potato gnocchi.

You can also substitute salt-cured chili paste if roasted Fresno chiles are not available.

(Continued)

Author Note: The remaining vegetable stock can be used to make the Sweet Corn Soup (page 22), or freeze it for a later use.

PARISIAN GNOCCHI

SERVES 4

1½ cups water

12 tablespoons (1½ sticks) salted butter

1 tablespoon salt

2 cups all-purpose flour, plus 2 cups for piping

1 cup freshly grated Parmesan cheese (see Contributor Notes)

⅛ teaspoon freshly grated nutmeg

5 large farm eggs

- Combine the water, butter, and salt in a medium-size heavy-bottomed pot over high heat. Bring to a boil, stirring occasionally. Watch carefully to be sure that the pot does not boil over or too much liquid does not evaporate, as changing the ratio of liquid to flour could make tough gnocchi.

- Once the liquid comes to a boil, add the flour and stir until the mixture forms a dough and pulls away from the sides of the pot. Add the cheese and nutmeg, then continue to stir until fully incorporated.

- Remove from the heat and transfer the dough to the bowl of a stand mixer fitted with a paddle attachment. Add the eggs one at a time while mixing on medium speed, mixing just until each egg is incorporated. At first the dough will look broken, but as you add the eggs it will come back together. Do not overmix.

- Once the mixture has become homogeneous again, turn off the mixer. Line two baking sheets with parchment and sift the 2 cups of flour generously onto the parchment paper. Transfer the dough to a piping bag without a tip. The dough should all fit in one bag, or piping it in batches is okay, too.

- Pipe the gnocchi onto the floured baking sheets into ¼-inch ropes until all is used. Refrigerate for about 30 minutes (to refrigerator temperature) to firm.

- In the meantime, fill a large pot partway with water and bring to a boil over high heat, adding salt until the water tastes like the ocean. In a very large bowl, prepare an ice bath using a ratio of 3 cups of ice to 6 cups of water. Set aside.

- Remove the gnocchi from the refrigerator one baking sheet at a time. Use a bench scraper to cut the ropes into 1- to 1½-inch-long segments, depending on your preference. Place the gnocchi in the pot of boiling water and cook until they float to the top, 2 to 3 minutes. Strain them out as they rise and shock them in the ice bath. Repeat until all the gnocchi are cut and cooked.

- Strain the gnocchi from the ice bath into a large mixing bowl, tossing with 3 tablespoons of blended oil to prevent sticking. Use the gnocchi within 3 to 4 days, or freeze for up to 2 weeks.

Contributor Notes: You can substitute a harder cheese for the Parmesan, such as Gruyère or pecorino.

You can also make the gnocchi to order, rather than blanching them in advance.

If you freeze the gnocchi, avoid stacking them. Laying them flat on a sheet is best.

GRILLED LOBSTER TAILS WITH SWEET CORN, CHERRY TOMATOES, AND BASIL

Executive chef **DAN SILVERMAN** | **THE STANDARD GRILL** New York, NY

SERVES 4

LOBSTER

6 (1¼-pound) lobsters (3 half tails per serving)

Sea salt

Freshly ground black pepper

Lobster Spice (recipe follows)

4 tablespoons (½ stick) unsalted butter, melted

CORN, CHERRY TOMATOES, AND BASIL

1 tablespoon olive oil

2 tablespoons unsalted butter

5 scallions, all the green parts and a little white, sliced finely

5 medium-size ears fresh white corn, husked, cleaned, kernels removed (about 4 cups)

Salt and freshly ground black pepper

12 cherry tomatoes, halved

8 basil leaves, cut in chiffonade, plus additional for garnish

While my family and I were in Maine this summer, we had lobsters and corn just about every day. A neighbor kept giving us tomatoes. . . . This great recipe has all of that. It incorporates white corn, ripe tomatoes, and fresh lobsters—and yet all of the dish's components can stand on their own. The corn-and-tomato salad is a great salad in its own right; the spice mix might also work well on pork; and, well, lobsters are great anytime, anywhere.

- Preheat a grill to medium-high heat.

- Bring an extra-large pot of salted water to a rolling boil over high heat. Drop in one lobster, head first. Cover and cook for 3 minutes (the lobster will not be fully cooked). Using tongs, transfer the lobster to a baking sheet. Return the water to a boil and repeat the above with the remaining lobsters.

- Cut the lobsters in half lengthwise and rinse them under water to clean them.

- Grill the lobsters, meat side down, for 6 to 8 minutes, or until the meat is fully cooked through. Remove the lobsters from the grill and let them cool enough to work with.

- Remove the tail meat from the shells and place on a baking sheet. Season each tail with sea salt, pepper, and a small pinch of lobster spice. Brush with the melted butter and set aside, covered with foil, until serving time.

- Remove the claw and knuckle meat (preferably using a lobster claw cracker) and set aside.

- To prepare the corn, cherry tomatoes, and basil, heat a nonstick pan over medium heat. Add the olive oil and butter. When the butter begins to foam, add the scallions and cook for 2 to 3 minutes, just until they wilt. Add the corn and sauté for 2 to 3 minutes. Season to taste with salt and pepper. Add the lobster claw and knuckle meat, toss gently to combine, and heat the lobster through, 2 to 3 minutes more. Add the cherry tomatoes and basil. Season to taste with salt and pepper.

- To serve, divide the corn and lobster mixture among four plates, then place the grilled lobster tails on top of the vegetables. Garnish with basil.

LOBSTER SPICE

MAKES ABOUT ¼ CUP

½ vanilla bean, dried well (See Contributor Note)
2 cinnamon sticks
1 teaspoon freshly grated nutmeg
4 teaspoons whole allspice
1 teaspoon cayenne
1 teaspoon granulated sugar
6 whole cloves

- Combine all the spices in a spice grinder and grind finely. Store in an airtight container in a cool, dark place for up to 3 months.

Contributor Note: Dry the vanilla bean for 25 to 30 minutes at 225°F.

CORN-POACHED HALIBUT WITH TOMATO
AND CHARRED JALAPEÑO CHUTNEY

Food stylist **BRIAN PRESTON-CAMPBELL** New York, NY

SERVES 4

2 jalapeños

1 teaspoon vegetable oil

2 tablespoons olive oil

1 teaspoon peeled and grated fresh ginger

½ medium-size Spanish onion, diced

1 ripe beefsteak tomato, diced

Juice of ½ lime

1 tablespoon minced fresh cilantro

Salt and freshly ground black pepper

2 tablespoons unsalted butter

2 large cloves garlic, minced

4 ears fresh sweet corn, husked, cleaned, kernels removed, cobs reserved (about 3 cups)

2-plus cups fish stock, low-sodium chicken broth, or water

Juice of ½ lemon

4 (6- to 8-ounce) fresh halibut fillets

The inspiration for this recipe—my wife, Rebecca—is a self-described corn addict. She adores it in almost any form: tamales, polenta, corn bread, tortillas, and roasted on the cob. I put together this recipe with her in mind, and added a few of her other loves, including onions, spicy jalapeños, and a superripe tomato. It was an instant hit, to say the least.

- To make the chutney, lightly oil the jalapeños with the vegetable oil and place them directly onto a gas stove burner (alternatively, place them onto a hot grill or under the broiler) and char on all sides, using long kitchen tongs to turn them. The skin will blister and turn black in some spots—this is desirable. Allow to cool slightly, then chop coarsely and set aside.

- Place the olive oil in a small saucepan over medium heat. Add the ginger and cook for 3 minutes, or until the ginger softens, but do not let it brown. Add the onion and sweat for an additional 10 minutes, or until translucent. Stir in the tomato, jalapeños, lime juice, and cilantro. Season with salt and pepper and cook just until barely heated through. Remove from the heat and set aside.

- In a 5-quart straight-sided skillet, melt the butter over medium heat, then add the garlic and sweat until lightly toasted, 1 to 2 minutes. Do not allow to burn. Add the corn kernels and cook for an additional 5 minutes, until the corn is tender. Add the corncobs (if they don't fit in the pan, break them in half) and the stock. Cover and bring to a boil. At the boil, lower the heat to a simmer and cook for 10 minutes.

(Continued)

- Remove the cobs from the pot and season the broth lightly with salt and pepper and the lemon juice. Pour half of this mixture into a blender. Puree until smooth and return to the pot. Adjust the thickness with a little more stock if necessary—it should be the consistency of thin soup. Leave the pot on low heat until ready to poach the fish.

- To poach the halibut, bring the reserved corn broth to a simmer. Season both sides of the fish with salt and pepper and carefully place the halibut into the liquid. Decrease the heat to low, cover, and allow the fish to poach for 8 to 10 minutes, or until fork-tender.

- Place each portion of halibut into a shallow bowl and cover with one-quarter of the poaching liquid. Spoon a few tablespoons of the chutney over the fish and serve with the remaining chutney on the side.

WARM POLENTA STEW

Chef–author **DANA JACOBI** | *12 BEST FOODS COOKBOOK* New York, NY

SERVES 4

2 teaspoons plus 2 tablespoons extra-virgin olive oil

¾ cup polenta (not instant)

3 cups boiling water

1 cup finely chopped Vidalia onion

1 clove garlic, chopped

1 (28-ounce) can plum tomatoes, drained

1 teaspoon dried oregano

2 sun-dried tomato halves, chopped finely

Salt and freshly ground black pepper

2 tablespoons grated Parmigiano-Reggiano cheese, for garnish

Using the prepared polenta sold in a tube is easy, but it does not compare with homemade. So I was thrilled when Chef Gary Danko, from San Francisco, shared his oven method for making creamy polenta without having to stand over a pot stirring it. One of my favorite ways to serve it is cubed and combined with a sun-dried tomato sauce to make this colorful stew.

- Preheat the oven to 350°F.

- In a medium-size cast-iron or other heavy, ovenproof pot, heat 2 teaspoons of the oil over medium-high heat. With a wooden spoon, mix in the polenta, stirring until it is coated with oil and hot to the touch, about 5 minutes. Lower the heat, if necessary, to avoid browning. Turn off the heat.

- Stand back and carefully whisk in the boiling water: The mixture will splutter and spatter. When the polenta is smoothly blended, season to taste with salt.

- Place the pot in the oven and bake, uncovered, for 45 minutes, until the polenta is thick and slightly grainy but tender to the bite.

- Coat a 9-inch square baking dish with extra-virgin olive oil or cooking spray. Pour the hot polenta into the prepared dish, scraping as much of it as you can from the pot. Smooth the polenta with a moistened rubber spatula to make an even layer. Set it aside to cool. If you are not making the stew immediately, cover the cooled polenta and refrigerate for up to 3 days.

(Continued)

- In a large, deep saucepan or small Dutch oven, heat the remaining 2 tablespoons of oil over medium-high heat. Sauté the onion and garlic until softened, about 5 minutes. Add the tomatoes, oregano, and sun-dried tomatoes. Season to taste with salt and pepper. Simmer until the tomatoes are soft but not mushy, about 15 minutes.

- Meanwhile, cut the polenta into 1-inch cubes. Add it to the sauce, stirring gently so the polenta holds its shape. Simmer just until the polenta is heated through. Serve sprinkled with the cheese.

ROASTED SALMON WITH
CORN SALAD AND SALSA VERDE

Executive chef–owner **GABRIEL RUCKER** | **LE PIGEON** Portland, OR

SERVES 4

CORN SALAD

2 tablespoons unsalted butter

1 oil-cured anchovy, smashed into a paste (optional)

¼ teaspoon chili flakes

¼ teaspoon mustard powder

2 medium-size ears fresh yellow corn, kernels removed (about 1½ cups)

Salt

3 scallions, white and green parts, chopped

6 boquerones, chopped roughly (optional) (see Author Notes)

4 red radishes, chopped

Juice of 1 lemon

1 tablespoon extra-virgin olive oil

Sea salt

Freshly ground black pepper

SALSA VERDE

1 bunch fresh Italian parsley, minced

1 bunch fresh oregano, minced

1 shallot, minced

¼ cup extra-virgin olive oil

Salt

This dish is light, flavorful, and delicious! Corn is an ingredient we love to use at Le Pigeon because it is so much more complex than people think. It is sweet, but it brings out great earthy flavors in the other foods it's cooked with. That is what we try to do at Le Pigeon—layer flavors so they really jump.

- Preheat the oven to 375°F.

- To make the corn salad, place the butter, anchovy if using, chili flakes, and mustard powder in a large sauté pan over medium heat and stir until the butter is melted. Add the corn, season with salt, and stir. Transfer the mixture to a baking sheet and roast in the oven for 20 minutes, or until the corn starts to brown on the edges. Let cool for 10 minutes.

- Place the corn, scallions, boquerones, and radishes in a large mixing bowl and toss well. Add the lemon juice and oil. Season with sea salt and black pepper. Set aside.

- To make the salsa verde, combine all the salsa ingredients in a medium-size bowl, mix well, and set aside.

- Preheat the oven to 400°F.

- To prepare the salmon, heat the oil in a wide sauté pan over medium-high heat until hot. Season the salmon fillets with salt and sear them presentation side down to make a nice crust, about 3 minutes.

- Transfer the fillets to a baking dish and roast them in the oven for 4 minutes.

SALMON

3 tablespoons canola oil,
   vegetable oil, or olive oil blend
4 (6-ounce) skinless salmon fillets
Sea salt
Juice of 1 lemon

- To serve, place the salmon fillets on plates and sprinkle with sea salt and a squeeze of lemon juice. Top with the corn salad, then drizzle the plate with salsa verde.

Contributor Note: Instead of sautéing the salmon, you can also poach it. In a metal baking dish, heat 2 cups of extra-virgin olive oil to 110°F. Season the salmon fillets with salt and submerge them in the oil. Let them poach in the oil for 10 to 14 minutes. Remove with a slotted spatula and transfer to a tray lined with paper towels.

Author Notes: Boquerones are white Spanish anchovies that can be found in any Spanish supermarket or in the ethnic section of high-end grocery or gourmet food stores.

If you don't care for anchovies, you can leave them out altogether and this dish will still be delicious!

PAN-SEARED BRANZINO
WITH CORN CHORIZO PUDDING
AND SMOKED TOMATO VINAIGRETTE

Chef **CANDY ARGONDIZZA** director of culinary arts **FRENCH CULINARY INSTITUTE** New York, NY

SERVES 8

SMOKED TOMATO VINAIGRETTE

12 plum tomatoes, halved

1 tablespoon ground cumin

2 tablespoons honey

1 tablespoon smoked paprika

6 cloves garlic, sliced thinly

2 ounces sherry vinegar

3 ounces corn oil combined with 3 ounces extra-virgin olive oil

Juice of 1 lemon

Salt and freshly ground black pepper

CORN CHORIZO PUDDING

4 cups cream

4 cups corn (about 5 medium-size ears) (see Contributor Notes)

Salt and freshly ground black pepper

4 whole large eggs

6 large egg yolks

4 ounces dried chorizo sausage, peeled, cubed into ¼-inch dice, rendered, and drained on a paper towel

In my thirty-two years of cooking, my culinary pursuit has always been to do high-quality, seasonal food that was simple and full of flavor. As a woman chef, I think we tend to think of food with simplicity and letting quality express itself without too much manipulation. This recipe reflects that for me. It's a great recipe that evokes all the best things about summer—corn, tomatoes, fish, and a smoky, all-American flavor. It's simple and doable for a home cook, and yet very sophisticated.

- Marinate the tomatoes with the cumin, honey, paprika, and garlic for 1 hour.

- Preheat the oven to 325°F with a rack in the center. Butter eight individual ramekins and set aside.

- Place 3½ cups of the cream and the corn in a medium-size saucepan over medium-high heat. Season with salt and pepper, bring to a boil, then shut off the heat but leave the pan on the stovetop. In a medium-size bowl, whisk together the whole eggs and yolks. Temper the eggs by slowly adding a little of the hot corn mixture (about ¼ cup) to them, whisking constantly. Pour the tempered egg mixture into the corn mixture and add the remaining ½ cup of cream to cool the mixture down. Continue whisking for 1 minute.

- Remove about ¼ cup of the whole corn kernels with a slotted spoon and set aside. Puree the remaining corn mixture in a blender to a smooth consistency and set aside.

BRANZINO

2 (2-pound) branzino (sea bass), filleted and pinboned, divided into 8 (4-ounce) portions

Salt and freshly ground black pepper

3 to 4 tablespoons vegetable oil (or enough to cover the surface of the sauté pan)

4 tablespoons (½ stick) unsalted butter

1 sprig fresh thyme

- Divide the rendered chorizo and reserved corn kernels evenly among the prepared ramekins. Pour the pureed corn mixture over the chorizo and corn, filling the ramekins three-quarters of the way up the sides.

- Place the ramekins into a large baking dish (you may have to use two to fit all of the ramekins) and pour hot water halfway up the sides of the ramekins. Bake until set, 40 to 45 minutes. Remove from the oven and decrease the temperature to 300°F. Let cool for at least 15 minutes, then unmold onto individual dinner plates and set aside.

- Transfer the tomatoes to a baking dish and gently roast for 1 hour to concentrate their flavors.

- Remove the tomatoes from the oven and puree in a blender, along with the sherry vinegar. While pureeing, slowly add the corn oil and blended oil to emulsify the mixture. Squeeze in the lemon juice. Season with salt and pepper to taste, then puree for another minute.

- To prepare the branzino, season the fillets with salt and pepper. Heat the oil in a wide sauté pan over medium-high heat until hot. Sear the fish skin side down until crisp and golden brown, 4 to 5 minutes. Decrease the heat to medium-low and cook for an additional 2 to 3 minutes, until the fleshy unseared part of the fish begins to warm up through the skin.

- Add the butter and thyme to the pan. Turn the fish and continue cooking, basting it with the butter and thyme, until done, 2 to 3 minutes. Season with salt and pepper to taste. Remove from the heat and set aside.

(Continued)

- To serve, place the fish on plates skin side up next to the unmolded corn pudding and add a spoonful of the smoked tomato vinaigrette to each plate.

Contributor Notes: Fresh corn is preferred, but canned or frozen is okay.

You can substitute any kind of bass for the branzino, such as black bass, wild striped bass, or even red snapper or tilefish.

SIDES

FRESH CORN AND BLACK BEAN SALAD

CARAMELIZED CORN WITH SHALLOTS

BAKED POLENTA WITH GORGONZOLA

ROASTED CORN WITH SMOKED BACON
AND CARAMELIZED VIDALIA ONIONS

CORN PUDDING WITH BACON AND LEEKS

CREAMED SWEET CORN WITH CORN BREAD CRUMBS

LATIN-STYLE CREAMED CORN

GRILLED CORN, MEXICAN STYLE

WARM CORN SOUFFLÉS

SPICY STIR-FRIED CORN AND BROCCOLI

YANKEE CORN BREAD

FRESH CORN AND BLACK BEAN SALAD

Food marketing consultant and educator **TERRY FRISHMAN** New York, NY

SERVES 8

6 medium-size ears fresh corn, boiled or roasted (about 4½ cups)

2 (14-ounce) cans black beans, drained and rinsed

½ red bell pepper, seeded and chopped coarsely

½ yellow bell pepper, seeded and chopped coarsely

½ green bell pepper, seeded and chopped coarsely

1 scallion, sliced on the rings, chopped on the greens

1 tablespoon green olive oil

3 cloves garlic, minced or pressed

¼ teaspoon ground cumin

Juice of 2 lemons (or limes, or one of each)

Sea salt

Freshly ground black pepper

My family loves black beans and fresh corn on the cob. I discovered a match made in heaven when I made this quick, delicious, and colorful recipe one day for my husband, Gary, and daughters Ivy and Becca. It's become a family classic. The amount and flavor can be adjusted based upon personal preference of how much corn, beans, pepper, and spices you want to use.

- Slice the corn kernels off the cobs into a large mixing bowl. Add the remaining ingredients and toss to mix. Season to taste with the salt and pepper, and serve.

Contributor Note: If you like heat, substitute minced jalapeño peppers for the scallion, or add some of your favorite hot sauce for a kick. You can also add chopped cilantro for extra flavor.

CARAMELIZED CORN WITH SHALLOTS

Chef–author **MARTHA STEWART** | *HEALTHY QUICK COOK*

SERVES 4

1 tablespoon unsalted butter

4 ears fresh corn, kernels removed (about 3 cups)

4 large shallots, cut into ¼-inch slices

Pinch of granulated sugar

Kosher salt and freshly ground black pepper

2 tablespoons fresh thyme leaves, plus 1 large sprig for garnish

I have taken much inspiration through the years from the hospitality of southern women. I like tasty, good, simple food, and that's what southern food is—just like this recipe. It's sweet, simple, and delicious! The caramelizing of the corn further enhances its natural sweetness, while the shallots balance it out with their delicate and savory flavor. Of course, fresh corn is best, but frozen will also work.

- In a large skillet over medium heat, melt the butter. Add the corn, shallots, sugar, and salt and pepper. Cook, stirring occasionally to prevent burning, until the corn is caramelized, about 5 minutes.

- Stir in the thyme and cook for 5 minutes more. Season with salt and pepper to taste. To serve, garnish with the sprig of thyme.

BAKED POLENTA WITH GORGONZOLA

Chef–author **CLAUDIA RODEN** | *THE FOOD OF ITALY: REGION BY REGION*

SERVES 4 TO 6

1⅔ cups cornmeal

6½ cups cold water

1 tablespoon salt

6 tablespoons unsalted butter

Freshly ground black pepper

½ pound Gorgonzola cheese, cut into ½-inch pieces or crumbled

Our nanny in Egypt was a Slovene Italian from a village in the region of Friuli in Italy. She used to make polenta, which still brings back fond memories. It is now very easy to make with the precooked variety we can buy today. This recipe is for an Italian classic, a delicious heartwarming winter dish. You can use other strong-tasting cheeses. It can be served as a main course, with a tossed salad and zesty red wine.

- Preheat the oven to 425°F. Butter a 9 by 9-inch ovenproof dish and set it aside.

- Combine the cornmeal and water in a very large saucepan and stir thoroughly. Add the salt, and stirring vigorously and constantly so that lumps do not form (this is crucial), bring to a boil over high heat. This should take 5 to 7 minutes, and the cornmeal should grow by more than a third.

- Decrease the heat to medium, continue to stir constantly, and cook for another 3 minutes.

- Stir in the butter. Add pepper to taste. Decrease the heat to medium low and continue to stir until the butter is completely melted, about 2 minutes.

- Pour a layer of hot polenta into the prepared baking dish. Cover with a layer of cheese pieces, then continue with another layer of polenta, another of cheese, and finish with polenta.

- Bake for 20 minutes. Increase the oven heat to 550°F and bake for another 5 minutes, until the top is slightly browned.

- Let cool for at least 15 minutes before serving.

ROASTED CORN WITH SMOKED BACON
AND CARAMELIZED VIDALIA ONIONS

Chef **BOB WAGGONER** | *UCOOK! WITH CHEF BOB* Charleston, SC

SERVES 4

6 large ears fresh corn, unhusked (see Author Notes)

2 to 3 tablespoons olive oil, or more as needed

2 large Vidalia onions, julienned

4 slices uncooked apple-smoked bacon, cut into medium dice

2 tablespoons sorghum syrup

1 tablespoon salted butter

Fresh chives, finely chopped, for garnish

Salt and freshly ground black pepper

After living in France for eleven years and cooking with some of the best chefs in the world, I learned one very valuable lesson: Some of the best food products come from within our own area. When I eventually came back to the United States and moved to Charleston, South Carolina, I insisted on American produce and American products. Corn is one of our main food sources in this country, and this recipe is a play on French Low Country cuisine. This dish will be a great addition to any meal you want to prepare. *Bon appétit!*

- Roast the corn in their husks on a preheated medium-hot grill (or in a preheated 400°F oven) for 30 to 40 minutes, or until charred. Remove from the heat and let cool. Remove the husks and cut the kernels from the cobs. Separate any chunks into individual kernels.

- Coat the bottom of a wide skillet with the oil and place it over medium-high heat, then add the onions. Spread out the onions evenly and cook for 30 to 45 minutes, or until they begin to brown and sweeten in flavor. Stir occasionally to keep them from burning, lowering the heat to medium if necessary. If the onions look as if they are drying out, add splashes of water. You may also want to add more oil after 20 to 30 minutes, to keep the onions completely coated.

- While the onions are cooking, render the bacon in a separate skillet over medium heat until well browned, 4 to 6 minutes. Drain the excess fat.

- Remove the onions from the heat and add the sorghum syrup. Stir in the bacon and corn and cook until heated through. Add the butter and chives and salt and pepper to taste.

Author Notes: All varieties of corn are delicious with this recipe—white, yellow, and bicolor.

This recipe also works without roasting the corn. Simply cut the raw kernels off the cobs, and when you add them to the pan with the onions and cooked bacon, cook the combination for slightly longer to ensure that the kernels are cooked through, 6 to 10 minutes.

Regular molasses works fine in this dish, too.

CORN PUDDING WITH BACON AND LEEKS

Private chef–author **JACKIE M. LEE** New York, NY

SERVES 4 TO 6

5 slices uncooked bacon, chopped roughly

1 tablespoon olive oil

3 ears fresh corn, kernels removed (2 to 2½ cups)

1 cup leeks, white part only, cleaned and chopped

1 clove garlic, chopped roughly

⅓ cup red bell pepper, seeded and diced small

Salt and freshly ground black pepper

Tabasco

2 cups heavy whipping cream

3 large egg yolks

½ teaspoon mustard powder

½ teaspoon Worcestershire sauce

½ tablespoon coarsely chopped fresh Italian parsley

½ tablespoon chopped fresh chives

When I cook, the flavors always start in my head. I usually pick a central ingredient and then build the dish from there. I love making this delectable and creamy corn pudding in the summer, when the corn is so fresh and sweet. The leeks and the bacon add the salty, smoky, and earthy elements to the dish, making this a great complement to any entrée. I usually find myself eating it all by itself, it's that good!

- Preheat the oven to 350°F. Spray an 8 by 8 by 2-inch casserole dish (or similar size) with nonstick cooking spray and set it aside.

- Sauté the bacon in a skillet over medium heat until crisp. Remove the bacon and drain on a paper towel.

- Drain two-thirds of the bacon fat out of the skillet and add the olive oil to the remaining bacon fat. Add the corn, leeks, garlic, and red bell pepper. Sauté over medium heat for about 5 minutes, or until all of the vegetables are just cooked.

- Remove the pan from the heat. Add the bacon bits and mix until well incorporated. Season with salt and pepper to taste, then season with the Tabasco to your preferred level of heat.

- In a large mixing bowl, mix together the cream, egg yolks, mustard powder, Worcestershire, parsley, and chives.

- Place the corn mixture in the bottom of the prepared baking dish and spread it out evenly. Pour the cream mixture over the top and bake for 55 minutes. Let cool slightly, about 5 minutes, then serve hot.

CREAMED SWEET CORN
WITH CORN BREAD CRUMBS

Executive chef **PETER VAUTHY** | **RED, THE STEAKHOUSE** Miami, FL

SERVES 6

2 tablespoons sweet cream butter

1 tablespoon sliced shallot

2 cloves garlic, sliced

8 medium-size ears corn, husked, cleaned, kernels removed, cobs reserved (about 6 cups)

4 cups heavy cream

½ tablespoon chopped fresh parsley

½ tablespoon chopped fresh chives

Kosher salt and freshly ground black pepper

1 cup corn bread crumbs (see Contributor Note)

This has become one of our signature dishes at Red South Beach. Coming from the Midwest, where sweet corn is enjoyed in the height of summer only, it was a welcome surprise to find succulent local sweet corn available all year round. We use the corncobs as the base for our corn cream, and we cut the corn to ensure the freshest product and the perfect accompaniment to our steaks.

- Preheat the oven to 350°F.

- Melt 1 tablespoon of the butter in a medium-size saucepan over medium heat. Add the shallot and garlic and sauté until soft, 3 to 5 minutes.

- Add the reserved corncobs and the heavy cream to the pan and bring to a simmer. Let the mixture simmer for 20 minutes, or until the cream is reduced by half. Remove the corncobs and discard. Reserve ½ cup of the cream. Discard the remaining cream, or save it for another use.

- Melt the remaining tablespoon of butter in a medium-size sauté pan. Add the corn and sauté for 3 to 5 minutes, or until it reaches your desired tenderness. Add the reserved ½ cup of corn cream, the parsley, and chives. Stir until evenly combined. Season with salt and pepper.

- Pour the mixture into an 8 by 8-inch ovenproof dish (or similar size) or 6 (6-ounce) individual ramekins. Top with the corn bread crumbs and bake until the crumbs are golden brown, about 10 minutes. Serve piping hot.

Contributor Note: Regular bread crumbs can be substituted if corn bread crumbs are not available.

LATIN-STYLE CREAMED CORN

Chef–restaurateur **ZACHARY BRUELL** | **PARALLAX RESTAURANT AND LOUNGE** Cleveland, OH

SERVES 4

4 tablespoons (½ stick) unsalted butter

3 tablespoons diced shallot

1 tablespoon diced garlic

1 teaspoon diced jalapeño (see Author Note)

6 medium-size ears fresh corn, kernels removed (about 4½ cups)

⅓ cup white-wine vinegar

2 cups heavy cream

¼ cup chopped fresh cilantro

Salt and freshly ground black pepper

This Latin-style creamed-corn recipe definitely has some zip to perk up your table. The corn and cilantro are a great combination for fresh summer dining. This is often on my menu at Parallax, teamed with fresh Costa Rican king clip. Complement this recipe at home with a French Rhône wine or your favorite California zinfandel.

- Melt the butter in a medium-size sauté pan over medium heat. Add the shallot and sauté lightly, about 2 minutes. Add the garlic and jalapeño and sauté until tender, about 2 minutes. Add the corn and continue to sauté for 2 minutes, or until the vegetables start to soften.

- Add the white-wine vinegar and deglaze the pan by scraping the bottom with a wooden spoon. Cook until the mixture reduces to a dry state, 5 to 7 minutes. Add the heavy cream and continue to cook until the mixture reduces by half, 10 to 15 minutes. Stir in the cilantro and season with the salt and pepper to taste. Serve warm.

Author Note: Leave the jalapeño seeds in for extra heat, or add another teaspoon of jalapeño.

GRILLED CORN, MEXICAN STYLE

Co-owner **LESLIE MEENAN | CAFÉ HABANA** New York, NY

SERVES 6

6 ears fresh corn, husked and cleaned

¾ cup freshly grated Cotija cheese (see Contributor Notes)

¾ teaspoon chile piquin (see Contributor Notes)

¼ cup mayonnaise, enough for a good smear on each cob

1 fresh lime, cut into 6 wedges, or more as desired

My rule of thumb with this recipe is that one can never have too much cheese. The chile piquin is really to taste. A healthy pinch is fine, but remember to wash your hands after touching it. I've made the mistake of wiping my eyes, and it stings like crazy! I recommend serving one wedge of lime per ear of corn. However, if your guests have gone nutty with the chile, they'll need more lime. Lime cuts the spiciness!

* Preheat a grill. When hot, place the husked corn directly on the grate and cook for about 10 minutes, turning frequently, or until the corn is browned.

* Meanwhile, mix the cheese and chile piquin on a platter big enough to roll your corn in it.

* When the corn is done cooking, take it off the grill and attach corn holders on each end. Frost the corn with the mayonnaise and then roll it in the cheese mixture.

* Serve immediately, garnished with the lime wedges.

Contributor Notes: You can substitute Pecorino Romano cheese for the Cotija cheese.

Chili powder can be used in place of the chile piquin.

WARM CORN SOUFFLÉS

Private chef–restaurant consultant **SCOTT BOVA** Westfield, NY

SERVES 6 TO 8

CORN VELOUTÉ

2 tablespoons unsalted butter

½ yellow onion, sliced thinly

1 rib celery, sliced thinly

2 cups fresh corn kernels (about 3 medium-size ears)

Salt

1 tablespoon fine yellow cornmeal

1 tablespoon all-purpose flour

1 cup Corn Stock (recipe follows)

SOUFFLÉS

1 tablespoon unsalted butter

4 large eggs, separated

2 tablespoons chopped fresh chives

Kosher salt

½ cup fresh corn kernels

⅓ cup finely grated Parmesan cheese

In any food I make, the flavors should explode on your palate; in this case, it is a delightful corn soufflé made of corn, corn, and more corn! My philosophy with food is: Take one ingredient, showcase it during its peak of perfection, and use every part of that product to show great respect for what nature offers. Try this corn soufflé as a side dish with a grilled steak, or add 6 ounces of lump crabmeat to the soufflé batter before baking for a great appetizer.

- To make the corn velouté, melt the butter in a medium-size saucepan. Add the onion and celery and sweat, covered, for about 10 minutes, or until very tender. Add the corn kernels and sweat, covered, for an additional 10 minutes. Season with salt to taste.

- Dust the mixture with the cornmeal and flour and cook for an additional 5 minutes, or until the flour is toasted and the aroma is nutty. Whisk in the corn stock and bring all the ingredients to a boil, stirring often to avoid burning. Simmer for 10 minutes. Season with salt to taste.

- Puree the mixture in a blender until very smooth. Strain through a fine sieve and reserve 1 cup. You will have extra velouté; reserve it to warm and serve with the soufflé.

- Preheat the oven to 400°F. Butter six or eight (4- to 6-ounce) individual ramekins and set them aside.

- Place the egg yolks in a medium-size saucepan. Whisk a small amount of the hot corn velouté into the egg yolks to temper them. Then add the yolks to the sauce, whisking well. Lower the heat to the lowest setting and cook for 3 to 5 minutes, keeping the sauce only warm; do not allow it to boil. Remove from the heat.

- In a medium-size bowl, beat the egg whites until they are stiff but not dry and form soft peaks. Add one-quarter of the egg whites to the corn velouté and mix. Fold the corn velouté into the egg whites. Add the fresh chives, taste, and season with salt as necessary.

- Fill a medium-size bowl halfway with ice and water and set it aside. Bring a small pot of water to a boil. Add the corn kernels to the boiling water, blanch for 1 minute, place in the ice bath to stop the cooking, then strain.

- Coat the sides of the prepared ramekins with the Parmesan cheese, allowing only what sticks to stay in the ramekin, discarding what falls out. Place 1 tablespoon of the blanched corn kernels in the bottom of each ramekin. Divide the soufflé batter among the ramekins, filling each about ½ inch from the top.

- Bake until golden brown, 12 to 15 minutes. Avoid opening the oven early, as the soufflés will fall. Serve immediately. Just before serving, pour a little extra corn velouté on top of the soufflés.

CORN STOCK

MAKES ABOUT 8 CUPS

2 ribs celery
1 medium-size yellow onion
1 leek, cleaned
3 cloves garlic
3 ears fresh corn, kernels removed
8 cups cold water

- Slice the celery, onion, leek, and garlic paper thin on a mandoline. Place them in a medium-size stockpot with the corncobs and water. Simmer over medium heat for 45 minutes. Remove from the heat and let sit at room temperature for 20 minutes. Drain the vegetables and cobs from the broth, and the stock is ready.

Contributor Note: The leftover stock is great to use in a corn risotto or a corn soup in place of chicken or vegetable stock.

SPICY STIR-FRIED CORN AND BROCCOLI

Chef–restaurateur **JEAN-GEORGES VONGERICHTEN | SPICE MARKET** New York, NY

SERVES 4

1 large stalk broccoli

2 tablespoons grapeseed, corn, or other neutral oil

1 cup fresh corn kernels (about 1 large ear) or whole baby corn (sliced in half if larger)

1 lemongrass stalk, trimmed and minced

1 fresh Thai chile, seeded and minced

1 clove garlic, minced

Soy sauce

Salt

The menu at Spice Market was inspired by the street food I enjoyed while traveling in Southeast Asia, much of which can be served family style, placed at the center of table for all to share. This particular recipe is especially simple and fun. You can use fresh baby corn, or if you have good local corn in summertime, you can cut that off of the cob for this dish. With Chinese technique and Thai flavors, it's a great side dish that pairs perfectly with grilled or roasted chicken and a chilled Alsatian Riesling!

- Cut the florets off of the broccoli and cut any large florets into 1-inch pieces. Peel the stem and cut at an angle into ⅛-inch-thick slices.

- Heat the oil in a wok or large skillet over high heat. When the oil is hot, add the broccoli and corn and stir-fry for about 1 minute. Add 3 tablespoons of water and continue to stir-fry until the broccoli is bright green and just tender, 3 to 4 minutes.

- Decrease the heat to medium and stir in the lemongrass, chile, and garlic. Continue to cook, stirring occasionally, until fragrant and tender, about 2 minutes.

- Season to taste with soy sauce and, if needed, salt and serve immediately.

YANKEE CORN BREAD

Executive Chef–owner **JONATHAN BENNETT | MOXIE THE RESTAURANT** Cleveland, OH

SERVES 8 (OR MORE)

⅔ stick unsalted butter

¾ cup granulated sugar

1 teaspoon salt

1 teaspoon vanilla extract

2 large eggs

2 cups all-purpose flour

¾ cup yellow cornmeal

¾ teaspoon baking powder

½ teaspoon baking soda

1⅓ cups buttermilk

Growing up in the South, we never used sugar in our corn bread. We introduced this interpretation to our customers at Moxie more than ten years ago, and it's been a staple ever since.

- Preheat the oven to 350°F with a rack in the center. Grease a 9 by 13-inch baking dish and set it aside.

- Combine the butter, sugar, and salt with a hand mixer or stand mixer fitted with beater attachments. Mix until light and fluffy. With the mixer on medium speed, add the vanilla and eggs one at a time and mix until completely incorporated.

- In a separate bowl, whisk together the flour, cornmeal, baking powder, and baking soda.

- With the mixer on low speed, add one-third of the dry ingredients and one-third of the buttermilk to the wet mixture and mix until everything is incorporated. Repeat two more times, until all of the ingredients are incorporated.

- Pour the batter into the prepared baking dish and bake for 25 to 30 minutes, or until golden brown on top. Remove from the oven, let cool slightly, and serve warm.

SWEETS

BLUEBERRY FINANCIER WITH CORN BREAD STREUSEL

CHOCOLATE PUDDING WITH CARAMEL PEANUT POPCORN
AND FRESH CORN SHERBET

STRAWBERRY CORN PONE WITH MAPLE CARAMEL

POACHED PEACHES AND RHUBARB WITH WARM CORN SHORTCAKES

CORNMEAL CAKE WITH HONEY AND BANANAS

FRESH CORN ICE CREAM

POPCORN PUDDING WITH SALTED CARAMEL CORN
AND BUTTERSCOTCH SAUCE

CORN CREMA WITH CHERRIES AND BOURBON CHANTILLY

BLUEBERRY FINANCIER
WITH CORN BREAD STREUSEL

Pastry chef **NICOLE KAPLAN** New York, New York

SERVES 8

STREUSEL

½ cup pecans

2 tablespoons brown sugar

1 tablespoon granulated sugar

½ teaspoon ground cinnamon

CAKE

8 tablespoons (1 stick) unsalted butter, at room temperature

½ cup plus 1 tablespoon granulated sugar

1 large egg

1 large egg yolk

1¼ cups cake flour

½ teaspoon baking powder

½ teaspoon baking soda

Pinch of salt

Seeds from 1 vanilla bean

½ cup plus 1 tablespoon crème fraîche

2 cups fresh blueberries

Corn Bread Streusel, for serving (recipe follows)

Warm Blueberries, for serving (recipe follows)

Corn Bread Ice Cream, for serving (recipe follows)

This dessert came to mind during a very hot summer a few years back, when the city had a huge blackout and I was very, very pregnant with my son. All I could think about was eating ice cream all day long. The hot summer days added in the thoughts of blueberries and corn. I would dream of eating this after a big lobster dinner, with lots of melted butter.

- Place the streusel ingredients in a food processor and grind to a rough powder. Set aside.

- Preheat the oven to 350°F with a rack in the middle.

- With a hand mixer or stand mixer fitted with a paddle attachment, cream the butter and sugar until soft and fluffy, about 5 minutes. Add the egg and egg yolk one at a time, mixing until incorporated. In a separate bowl, whisk together the flour, baking powder, baking soda, salt, and vanilla bean seeds. Alternating in three additions, add the combined dry ingredients and the crème fraîche, mixing just until each addition is incorporated.

- Layer half of the cake batter in an 8-inch square cake pan lined with parchment paper, or similar. Spread the blueberries on top in a neat layer. Sprinkle with half of the streusel. Carefully spread the remaining half of the cake batter and top with the remaining streusel. Bake until the cake springs back in the center, 25 to 30 minutes. Remove from the oven and let cool on a rack. Once it is cooled completely, cut into squares.

- To serve, place a piece of the warm cake in the center of a plate. Place some Corn Bread Streusel around the cake. Top it with the warm blueberries and a scoop of corn bread ice cream. Serve immediately.

CORN BREAD STREUSEL

MAKES ABOUT 1 CUP

½ cup freeze-dried corn (See Contributor Notes)
½ cup almond flour
1 teaspoon cake flour
Pinch of salt
6 tablespoons unsalted butter, melted

- Preheat the oven to 200°F with a rack in the middle.
- Place the corn, both flours, and the salt in a food processor and process until powdery. Drizzle in the butter and continue blending for about 1 minute. Transfer to a standard half sheet pan (18 by 13 inches) or similar. Bake until toasty but still light in color, 7 to 10 minutes. This streusel can be stored at room temperature for up to a week in an airtight container, or frozen for an extended period of time and then gently retoasted for a few minutes before using, to refresh the flavor.

WARM BLUEBERRIES

MAKES ABOUT 4 CUPS

4 cups fresh blueberries
½ cup confectioners' sugar
Seeds from 1 vanilla bean

- Combine all the ingredients in a large pan over medium heat. Cook until the berries start to give off a little juice and are glossy. Do not let them pop. They are best made right before serving, but they can be made earlier in the day and then heated. Do not make them any further in advance.

CORN BREAD ICE CREAM

MAKES ABOUT 2½ QUARTS

2 cups frozen corn (see Contributor Notes)
4 cups whole milk
2 cups heavy cream
½ cup plus ¾ cup granulated sugar
10 large egg yolks
¾ tablespoon salt

- Place the corn in a large pot over medium heat and heat it to evaporate any water from the freezer. Add the milk, cream, and ½ cup of the granulated sugar and bring to a boil.

- Place the remaining ¾ cup of sugar, the yolks, and salt in a medium-size bowl and whisk together. Gently temper the eggs by pouring the hot liquid into the bowl slowly, stirring constantly.

- Blend the mixture with an immersion blender until smooth. Strain and let cool.

- Freeze in an ice-cream maker according to its manufacturer's instructions.

Contributor Notes: You can buy freeze-dried fruits and veggies at Whole Foods, most major groceries. and health-food stores.

Fresh corn is okay to use, but then it's not necessary to heat it over medium heat to dry off the water.

CHOCOLATE PUDDING WITH CARAMEL PEANUT POPCORN AND FRESH CORN SHERBET

Pastry chef **LAURIE JON MORAN** New York, NY

SERVES 6

½ cup chopped dark chocolate

¾ cup whole milk

¾ cup heavy cream

4 large egg yolks

1½ tablespoons granulated sugar

Pinch of salt

Caramel Peanut Popcorn, for serving (recipe follows)

Corn Sherbet, for serving (recipe follows)

Like many of the desserts I've created throughout my career, this is a combination of three recipes that can be served separately and thoroughly enjoyed, although the combination of flavors when you serve them together is absolutely amazing. This particular combination expands on the flavor profile of the caramel peanut popcorn. The corn sherbet lightens the dish and adds a cold element, and the chocolate pudding adds unctuousness and creaminess, which plays against the crunchy saltiness of the candied corn and peanuts.

- Place the chocolate in a small heatproof or microwave-safe bowl. Either place the bowl on top of a pot filled partway with hot water and stir to melt the chocolate, or microwave for just a few seconds at a time, stirring often, until melted.

- In a small pot over medium heat, bring the milk and cream to a boil and then turn off the heat.

- Meanwhile, in a medium-size bowl, beat together the egg yolks and sugar until light and fluffy, 2 to 3 minutes. Whisk approximately one-third of the hot milk mixture into the egg mixture to temper the yolks, then slowly return that mixture to the pot with the rest of the milk mixture, whisking constantly. Stir in the salt.

- Cook over medium-low heat, stirring constantly, until the mixture starts to thicken and coats the back of a spoon, 10 to 12 minutes. Strain through a fine-mesh sieve onto the melted chocolate and blend with an immersion blender for about 2 minutes, or until it reaches a silky-smooth consistency. Refrigerate overnight in a tightly sealed container.

- To serve, place a portion of chocolate pudding in individual serving bowls, cover it with caramel peanut popcorn, and top with a scoop of corn sherbet.

CARAMEL PEANUT POPCORN

¾ cup granulated sugar
1¼ tablespoons unsalted butter
1 teaspoon fleur de sel
¼ cup peanuts, roasted
3½ cups popped corn (about 2 tablespoons unpopped kernels)

- Lightly grease the inside of a large bowl and the head of a spatula with nonstick cooking spray. The bowl should be large enough that the popcorn only fills it by one-third. Line a baking sheet with parchment paper.
- Place the sugar and butter in a small pot over medium heat and cook, stirring frequently, until it becomes a golden brown caramel, 8 to 10 minutes. Mix the fleur de sel and peanuts into the caramel mixture.

- Pour the mixture over the popcorn. Quickly, but carefully and gently, use the spatula to mix the popcorn and caramel, then pour the mixture onto the prepared baking sheet, keeping the popcorn pieces as separate as possible.
- Let cool to room temperature, then store in a tightly sealed container for up to 3 weeks.

CORN SHERBET

2½ cups whole milk
4 tablespoons (½ stick) unsalted butter
1¾ tablespoons honey
½ cup granulated sugar
⅓ cup fat-free milk powder
⅔ cup fresh corn kernels (about 1 small ear)

- In a medium-size pot over medium-low heat, heat the milk, butter, and honey until just warm.
- In a small bowl, mix together the sugar and milk powder, then whisk into the milk mixture until the milk powder has dissolved, about 30 seconds. Add the corn and bring to a boil, stirring occasionally. Take off the heat and let cool for about 1 hour.

(Continued)

- When the mixture is approximately 100°F (body temperature), blend with an immersion blender for several minutes, until the corn kernels have broken down and released their flavor. This will also emulsify the milk and butter into one homogenous liquid.

- Refrigerate overnight. Pour the mixture through a fine-mesh sieve, then freeze according to your ice-cream maker's manufacturer's directions.

Contributor Note: For a delicious snack or appetizer, omit the fleur de sel and instead add 2 tablespoons of crumbled fried smoked bacon.

Author Note: For the corn sherbet, the milk powder can be completely eliminated and the recipe still works very well.

STRAWBERRY CORN PONE
WITH MAPLE CARAMEL

Executive chef **RICHARD HETZLER** | **NATIONAL MUSEUM OF THE AMERICAN INDIAN'S MITSITAM CAFÉ**, Washington, DC

SERVES 8

1¾ cups pure maple syrup

3¼ cups heavy cream

10 tablespoons unsalted butter

2 cups fresh or frozen strawberries, sliced, plus additional for garnish

1 teaspoon ground cinnamon

1½ cups yellow cornmeal

Fresh whipped cream, for garnish

Extremely popular in the southern United States, corn pone is traditionally an eggless corn bread that is shaped into small ovals and fried or baked. This recipe puts our twist on corn pone by incorporating cream and berries, making it into a delicious dessert more closely reminiscent of warm porridge or bread pudding. I was first inspired to write this recipe thinking of my mom's fresh strawberry shortcakes being served warm from the oven.

- Pour 1 cup of the maple syrup into a medium-size saucepan over high heat and bring it to a rolling boil, 3 to 5 minutes. Turn off the heat and slowly whisk in ½ cup of the heavy cream. Be careful because the cream will boil up rapidly at first. Continue whisking until the mixture is smooth and all of the cream is incorporated. Whisk in 6 tablespoons of the butter, then turn off the heat and set aside.

- In a medium-size saucepan over medium heat, melt 2 tablespoons of the butter and add 1 cup of the sliced strawberries. Sauté for 7 to 9 minutes, or until the strawberries start to break down. Add the remaining ¾ cup of maple syrup, the remaining 2¾ cups of heavy cream, and the cinnamon. Bring to a boil.

- Slowly whisk in the cornmeal until incorporated, then lower the heat by half. Cook, stirring, for 6 to 8 minutes, or until the cornmeal is fully cooked. Remove from the heat and stir in the remaining 2 tablespoons of butter and the strawberries until incorporated.

- To serve, place a large spoonful of the strawberry pone in a bowl and top with 1 to 2 tablespoons of the maple caramel. Serve warm, garnished with fresh whipped cream and fresh strawberries as desired.

POACHED PEACHES AND RHUBARB
WITH WARM CORN SHORTCAKES

Pastry chef **COLLEEN GRAPES** | **THE HARRISON** New York, NY

SERVES 6

PEACHES

3 cups water

3 cups sweet white wine

2 cups granulated sugar

4 medium-size peaches

RHUBARB

1 cup granulated sugar

¾ cup honey

2 cups freshly squeezed orange juice

2 cups water

1 stalk lemongrass

1½ pounds rhubarb, sliced into 2-inch pieces, green parts discarded

½ cinnamon stick

I love to make these biscuits, which can be paired with beautiful, ripe peaches and bright, ruby rhubarb from some of my favorite New York City greenmarkets in the summer! Be creative and add spices and herbs. Take out the whipped cream and use ice cream. Use beautiful ripe fruits, or stew dried fruits. Make it your own, do it with love! When serving, I like to use a bowl so you can scoop up the juices, but use whatever plate you like best.

- Make the peaches: In a medium-size saucepot over high heat, bring the water, white wine, and sugar to a quick, rolling boil. Turn off the heat and let cool for 15 minutes.

- Use a paring knife to score the tops of the peaches, then place them in a separate large pot. Cover them with the poaching liquid until they float. Discard the remaining poaching liquid. Place a clean, thoroughly wet kitchen towel on top of the peaches in the liquid. This helps them stay submerged without touching the bottom of the pot.

- Place the pot on a low heat (do not let boil). Poach until just tender when stuck with a toothpick. Turn off the heat and let the peaches cool in the liquid to about room temperature.

- Remove the peaches and reserve the liquid. Remove the skins and slice into ½-inch slices. Store the slices in the liquid so they can be served at room temperature.

- Preheat the oven to 350°F.

CORN SHORTCAKES

1½ cups all-purpose flour

½ cup yellow cornmeal

5 tablespoons granulated sugar, plus some for sprinkling over the shortcakes

1 tablespoon plus 1 teaspoon baking powder

4 tablespoons (½ stick) unsalted butter

1¼ cups heavy cream

½ cup fresh corn kernels, cooked (about 1 small ear)

WHIPPED CREAM

2 cups heavy cream, kept cold

- To prepare the rhubarb, combine the sugar, honey, orange juice, and water in a medium-size bowl.

- Smash the lemongrass stalk with the back of a knife, then cut into 3-inch pieces. Place the rhubarb, cinnamon, and lemongrass into a medium-size ovenproof saucepan. Pour in the orange-juice mixture.

- Cover the saucepan with aluminum foil and place in the oven until the rhubarb is tender, about 40 minutes. Leave the oven on. Remove the foil, let cool, and discard the lemongrass and cinnamon stick. Refrigerate until needed.

- To make the shortcakes, place the flour, cornmeal, sugar, baking powder, and butter in a large bowl. With your hands, press, pinch, and fold everything together until *just* incorporated.

- Add the heavy cream and corn kernels and mix until the dough just forms a ball. Place on a lightly floured surface and knead a few times just to make sure it is completely combined.

- Press out the dough on a lightly floured surface so it is 1¼ to 1½ inches thick. Using a biscuit cutter or cookie cutter (in the shape that makes you happiest), cut the dough and place the shapes 3 inches apart on a baking sheet lined with parchment paper. Reshape the remaining dough and cut more until you use all of the dough.

- Sprinkle a little sugar on top of the shortcakes before they go into the oven. Bake for 20 to 25 minutes, or until lightly golden brown on the edges. The centers should be slightly fluffy to the touch, or you can insert a toothpick. If it comes out with just a few crumbs, the shortcakes are done.

(Continued)

- Let the shortcakes cool until just warm.

- Meanwhile, make the whipped cream by pouring 1½ cups of the heavy cream into a stand mixer fitted with the whisk attachment and whip on high speed until stiff peaks begin to form. Keeping the mixer on high, count to five and then turn it off. This mixes the cream to just slightly beyond stiff peaks.

- To serve, cut each shortcake in half. Pour about 2 tablespoons of poaching liquid from the rhubarb on the bottom half of each. Place pieces of rhubarb on the shortcake, using enough to form a layer. Then layer a dollop of whipped cream. Then place enough peaches on top of the cream to form another layer. Add more cream. Repeat the layers once more. Place the top of the shortcake on top and dust with a little confectioners' sugar.

- In a small bowl, combine the remaining ½ cup heavy cream, 2 tablespoons of the rhubarb poaching liquid, and 2 tablespoons of the peach poaching liquid. Make sure the poaching liquids are still very warm, or reheat if necessary. This makes a sauce to pour around your dessert, provided you haven't already eaten it!

CORNMEAL CAKE
WITH HONEY AND BANANAS

Consulting chef **EVE NASETTI** Boca Raton, FL

SERVES 8

1½ cups yellow cornmeal

2½ teaspoons baking powder

⅛ teaspoon salt

½ cup plus 6 tablespoons (1¾ sticks) unsalted butter, room temperature

¼ cup clover honey

½ cup plus 2 tablespoons granulated sugar

3 large egg whites

2 large ripe bananas

Whipped cream, for garnish

Fresh strawberries, for garnish

I created this recipe many years ago for the Jewish Holiday Cooking class that I taught at the Jewish Studies Center in Washington, DC. It is a great alternative dessert to the traditional honey cake.

- Preheat the oven to 350°F and place a rack in the middle. Grease a 9- or 10-inch springform pan.

- In a medium-size bowl, combine the cornmeal, baking powder, and salt.

- Place the butter in a separate bowl. Using a hand mixer or a stand mixer fitted with a paddle attachment, beat the butter on medium speed until light and fluffy. Continue beating while gradually adding the honey and ½ cup of the sugar.

- Stir all of the butter mixture into the cornmeal mixture.

- Using clean, dry beaters or a stand mixer fitted with a whisk attachment, beat the egg whites until stiff but not dry. Continue beating while gradually adding the remaining 2 tablespoons of sugar.

- Use a spatula to gently and gradually fold the beaten egg whites into the cornmeal mixture. Make sure the egg whites are completely incorporated without overmixing. Spoon half of the batter into the prepared springform pan, spreading it out evenly over the bottom of the pan.

- Slice the bananas into ¼-inch-thick, round slices. Place the slices over the batter in the pan. Do not overlap the bananas, but place them close to one another so as to make a thin layer of bananas. Carefully spoon the remaining batter over the bananas, so as not to move the bananas.

- Bake for 40 minutes, or until deep golden brown. The cake will pull away from the sides of the pan. Remove from the oven and let cool at room temperature. The cake will fall as it cools.

- Serve at room temperature, garnished with whipped cream and strawberries.

Author Note: Any flat-sided pan will work with this recipe, though springform is best for the nicest presentation.

FRESH CORN ICE CREAM

Founding pastry chef **ALLEN STAFFORD** | **CASELLULA** New York, NY

SERVES 4 TO 6

2 cups half-and-half

1 cup fresh corn kernels, cut from the cobs, including any juices (about 1 large ear)

2 corncobs, broken or cut into 2-inch pieces

5 large egg yolks

½ cup turbinado sugar

2 tablespoons chestnut honey (see Contributor Notes)

Pinch of kosher salt

⅛ teaspoon cayenne (see Contributor Notes)

Chopped chocolate, or chopped tomatoes, or fresh blueberries, for serving

I was born in North Carolina, and moved all around the South while growing up. The rituals of sharing a platter of corn on the cob and making ice cream from fresh summer fruit always felt like going back home for summer break, no matter how far from the grandparents we were. This ice cream blends two homey memories into one summery adventure, and, of course, it's best when corn is in season. Don't throw out the cobs after cutting the corn from them: They are just more corn goodness when steeped in the custard! You could substitute frozen corn and/or skip the cobs, but I don't recommend canned corn for this recipe. The natural starch in the corn acts as a thickener when it is heated, which makes the texture so silky and rich!

- In a medium-size saucepan over high heat, bring the half-and-half, corn kernels, and cob pieces to a boil. When the mixture starts to boil, remove from the heat immediately, and let infuse for 30 minutes, stirring occasionally.

- Meanwhile, in a large bowl, whisk together the egg yolks and sugar until the yolks are pale yellow. Whisk in the honey, salt, and cayenne.

- Remove the cobs from the corn mixture and discard them. With an immersion blender, or in a food processor, puree the corn mixture.

- Bring a large pot filled halfway with water to a simmer over low heat. Set the large bowl with the egg yolk mixture over the simmering water and slowly drizzle the corn mixture into the yolk mixture, stirring constantly, to make corn custard. Continue to stir the custard until it coats the back of a spoon, about 10 minutes. Turn off the heat and remove the bowl from the pot.

- Press plastic wrap onto the surface of the custard to avoid forming a skin. Chill in the refrigerator overnight, or for at least 4 hours. Warm custard will not freeze properly.

- Strain the custard through a fine-mesh sieve to remove the corn and any egg solids. Freeze in an ice-cream maker according to its manufacturer's directions.

- For a soft-serve consistency, eat immediately. Transfer to a freezer-safe container and freeze overnight for firmer ice cream.

- Garnish with the chopped chocolate, chopped tomatoes, or fresh blueberries. It's also delicious with sweet corn muffins!

Contributor Notes: I use chestnut honey to stabilize the sugar. You can use any honey, or even corn syrup, but I like the complex flavors of chestnut honey. It also enriches the color a bit.

Don't skip the cayenne! I add cayenne to many dishes, because the natural stimulants in it raise and sensitize your taste buds, making you literally *taste more*. I like to boost flavor when it's as subtle as corn. Plus, very cold foods such as ice cream numb your taste buds a bit. In very small amounts like this you may not even taste cayenne; it has more heat than flavor.

POPCORN PUDDING WITH SALTED CARAMEL CORN AND BUTTERSCOTCH SAUCE

Chef–owner **AMANDA COHEN** | **DIRT CANDY** New York, NY

SERVES 6

2 large eggs

1 tablespoon canola oil

¼ cup unpopped popcorn kernels

4 cups whole milk

1 cup corn kernels, frozen or fresh (about 1 large ear)

¾ cup plus 2 tablespoons granulated sugar

½ cup cornstarch

8 tablespoons (1 stick) butter

¼ fresh vanilla bean, seeds scraped

Butterscotch Sauce, for serving (recipe follows)

Salted Caramel Corn, for garnish (recipe follows)

This recipe is the creation of Debbie Lee, who was my pastry chef when I opened Dirt Candy. Almost all of the recipes on our menu have changed since she left, but this one remains, and it's still one of our most popular desserts.

- Beat together the eggs, then remove a quarter of the mixture (about 1 tablespoon) and discard it.

- Place the oil and popcorn kernels in a medium-size pot. Heat over medium-high heat until all of the kernels pop. Keeping the pot covered and peeking as needed will prevent making a mess! Remove any unpopped kernels.

- In the same pot, add the milk and corn and lower the heat to low. Let the mixture cook for 30 minutes, covered.

- In a separate bowl, whisk together the sugar, cornstarch, and eggs.

- To temper the eggs, whisk 2 tablespoons of the corn mixture into the egg mixture. Repeat the process 2 tablespoons at a time until the temperatures of the egg mixture and the corn mixture are approximately equal. You will probably have to whisk in a total of about ½ cup of the corn mixture to get them equal.

- Slowly whisk your warm egg mixture into the pot with your corn. Increase the heat to medium-low.

- Add the butter and the vanilla bean pod and seeds. Continually stir until the mixture thickly coats the back of a spoon, 10 to 12 minutes.

(Continued)

- Remove from the heat and press through a chinois or fine-mesh strainer. Discard the vanilla bean pod. Chill for about 4 hours before serving.

- To serve, rewhisk the pudding to break it up. Spoon the pudding into six individual ramekins. Drizzle the butterscotch sauce over the top, then garnish with a piece of caramel popcorn.

Contributor Note: You can combine the caramel corn and the pudding or serve them next to each other and let your guests combine them.

BUTTERSCOTCH SAUCE

MAKES ABOUT I CUP

2 tablespoons unsalted butter
½ cup firmly packed light brown sugar
⅓ cup heavy cream
Pinch of salt
1½ teaspoons vanilla extract

- Place the butter, sugar, and cream in a small pot and bring to a boil over medium-low heat, whisking constantly to incorporate, about 15 minutes. Remove from the heat, and stir in the salt and vanilla. Cool for at least 10 minutes, or until room temperature. The sauce can be stored tightly covered for up to 2 weeks.

SALTED CARAMEL CORN

MAKES 5 CUPS

1 tablespoon canola oil
¼ cup unpopped popcorn kernels
4 tablespoons (½ stick) unsalted butter
¾ cup firmly packed light brown sugar
¼ cup light corn syrup
¼ teaspoon vanilla extract
¼ teaspoon baking soda
¼ teaspoon kosher salt
¾ cup chopped, toasted, skinless hazelnuts (optional)
⅛ teaspoon fleur de sel

- Spray a baking sheet with nonstick spray or place a Silpat liner on it.

- Place the oil and popcorn kernels in a medium-size pot. Heat over medium-high heat until all of the kernels pop. Keeping the pot covered and peeking as needed will prevent making a mess! Remove any unpopped kernels.

- Attach a candy thermometer to a small pot. Add the butter, sugar, and corn syrup and bring to a boil on low heat. *Do not stir.*

- When it reaches 300°F, remove it from the heat immediately and stir in the vanilla, baking soda, and kosher salt. Pour the mixture over your popcorn and stir to coat. Add the hazelnuts, if using, and continue to stir until everything is evenly mixed.

- Use a spatula to spread the popcorn mixture on the prepared baking sheet. It will cool down very, very fast, so spread it to the edges as quickly as possible. It does not have to be entirely even. After you've spread the popcorn, and while still warm, sprinkle the fleur de sel over the top.

- Cool, then break into pieces. The caramel popcorn can be stored in an airtight container for up to 3 weeks.

CORN CREMA WITH CHERRIES AND BOURBON CHANTILLY

Consulting pastry chef **PICHET ONG** | **COPPELIA** New York, NY

SERVES 6

1½ cups whole milk

½ cup fresh corn kernels (about 1 small ear; frozen is okay, too)

1¼ teaspoons salt

⅓ cup plus 2 tablespoons granulated sugar

5 large egg yolks

1 large egg

1½ cups heavy cream

⅛ teaspoon freshly ground black or white pepper

2 tablespoons bourbon (see Author Notes)

15 whole fresh sweet red Bing cherries, pitted and halved

Pinch of salt

I have fond childhood memories of enjoying corn as a topping for an ice-cream sandwich, served on a scoop of coconut ice cream, on a hot-dog bun, off a food cart. As an adult, and pastry chef, I use corn in a whole variety of ways. This is one I'm particularly fond of, and it has traveled with me through different themes for which I've conceived menus—from steakhouse and seasonal American to Asian street food and the Latin comfort diner at Coppelia.

- In a medium-size pot, bring the milk, corn, salt, and ⅓ cup of the sugar to a simmer over low heat. Remove from the heat, cover, and infuse for at least 1 hour.

- Pour the mixture into a blender and process on high speed until very smooth.

- Whisk together the egg yolks, 1 whole egg, and 1 cup of the cream in a large bowl. Slowly whisk in the corn-infused milk. Strain through a fine-mesh sieve, pushing as much liquid through the sieve as possible. Stir in the pepper and 1 tablespoon of the bourbon. Chill completely, about an hour, to room temperature.

- Preheat the oven to 300°F.

- Divide the custard among 6 (6-ounce) ramekins, leaving about ¾ inch of space at the top for garnish. Set the ramekins in a deep baking dish and add hot tap water to the dish until it reaches halfway up the sides of the ramekins. Cover the baking dish with a flat-bottomed baking sheet or aluminum foil. Bake until the custards are firm around the sides with a small jiggly center the size of a dime,

65 to 75 minutes. Cool the custards completely in the baking pan, then refrigerate for at least 4 hours before serving.

- Just before serving, whip the remaining ½ cup of cream until it forms soft peaks. Add the pinch of salt, the remaining 2 tablespoons of sugar, and 1 tablespoon of bourbon. Continue whipping until it forms medium-size peaks. Spoon a dollop of whipped cream on top of each ramekin of crema, and garnish each with five cherry halves.

Author Notes: This is a great dessert to make ahead of time. Just garnish with the whipped cream and cherries when you're ready to serve.

If you want less of the liquor flavor, simply leave the remaining bourbon out of the whipped cream.

CONTRIBUTORS' BIOGRAPHIES

HUGH ACHESON

Hugh Acheson is the chef–partner of Five and Ten, the National, and Gosford Wine in Athens, Georgia, and Empire State South in Atlanta, Georgia. Born and raised in Ottawa, Canada, his experience includes working under Chef Rob MacDonald at the renowned Henri Burger restaurant in Ottawa, in San Francisco as the chef de cuisine with Chef Mike Fennelly at Mecca, and later as opening sous chef with famed chef Gary Danko at his namesake restaurant.

Chef Acheson's fresh approach to southern food has earned him a great deal of recognition, including *Food & Wine*'s Best New Chef (2002), the *Atlanta Journal Constitution* Restaurant of the Year (2007), a five-time James Beard nominee for Best Chef Southeast (2007, 2008, 2009, 2010, 2011) and a 2007 Rising Star from StarChefs.com. Chef Mario Batali chose Hugh as one of the 100 contemporary chefs in Phaidon Press's *Coco: 10 World Leading Masters Choose 100 Contemporary Chefs*. He also has his own cookbook, *A New Turn in the South: Southern Flavors Reinvented for Your Kitchen*.

CANDY ARGONDIZZA

After graduating top of her class at the Culinary Institute of America in 1981, Chef Candy Argondizza embarked on a twenty-year adventure cooking in restaurants all over New York City. She has landed herself appearances on the *Today* show, and invitations to the James Beard House. In 2001, she joined the French Culinary Institute's esteemed list of colleagues as a chef instructor. Candy is now the director of the culinary program at the French Culinary Institute, where she trains the industry's future chefs.

DAN BARBER

In May 2000, Dan opened Blue Hill restaurant with family members David and Laureen Barber. Since then, he has received numerous accolades, including the James Beard Awards for Best Chef: New York City (2006) and Outstanding Chef (2009). Recently appointed to the President's Council on Physical Fitness, Sports and Nutrition, Dan continues the work that he began as a member of Stone Barns Center for Food and Agriculture's board of directors, regarding food and agricultural policy. In 2009, he was named one of the world's most influential people in *Time* magazine's annual "Time 100."

ANDREW BEER

Chef Andrew Beer is the executive sous chef for Jean-Georges Vongerichten's Market in Boston. Born and raised in southeastern Massachusetts by a family that enjoyed cooking, he has fond memories of bacon and egg sandwiches, crispy cod cakes, and even chicken wings that made cooking an easy decision from an early age.

After graduating from the Culinary Institute of America, Chef Beer went on to work at such restaurants as the late Bay Tower Room in Boston, Massachusetts; the Wildflower in Vail, Colorado; and the Equinox in Manchester Center, Vermont. Eventually he went back to Boston to the kitchens of Aquitaine Bis and Upstairs on the Square. After a brief stint with the Dreamshop Hospitality Group, he became part of the opening team at Market in the W Hotel.

JONATHAN BENNETT

Jonathan Bennett is executive chef and partner of Moxie, the Restaurant, and Red, the Steakhouse, in Cleveland, Ohio, specializing in American Bistro cuisine. Moxie won the *Santé* magazine award in the Sustainability category in 2010. Red has been named one of the top ten steakhouses in the country by *Playboy* and *Esquire* magazines, and both restaurants have won numerous awards in *Cleveland Magazine*. A graduate of the Culinary Institute of America and native of North Carolina, Jonathan has served as sous chef at the Homestead in Hot Springs, Virginia; Plaza 600 in Cincinnati, Ohio; and Classics in Cleveland, Ohio.

J. TYLER BENTINE

Columbus, Ohio–born Tyler Bentine fell into cooking during college. He took a job frying chicken wings and bartending while studying business at Miami University in Oxford, Ohio. After graduation, he continued to bartend and cook at the local country club, where he eventually ran the kitchen. He went on to study at the Culinary Institute of America in New York, during which he had an externship at the Red Fish Grill under Chef Brian Katz. He continues to cook private events in the area, awaiting graduation at the end of 2011. Tyler plans to move to Chicago to further pursue his culinary career.

MICHELLE BERNSTEIN

A Miami native of Jewish and Latin descent, Michelle Bernstein has dazzled diners and critics alike with her sublime cuisine. "My food is luxurious but approachable," says Chef Bernstein, a James Beard Award–winner (Best Chef South 2008) and author of *Cuisine a Latina*.

Chef Bernstein has two successful Miami outposts, Michy's and SRA. Martinez, which she owns and operates with her partner–husband, David Martinez, as well as a location at the Omphoy in Palm Beach County, Florida. She recently launched the Miami chapter of Common Threads, an after-school program dedicated to teaching underprivileged kids ages eight through eleven to cook, socialize, and eat healthy.

TAIDED BETANCOURT

Taided Betancourt grew up in a family of food lovers, where food was the center of every celebration and everyone pitched in. It was during college that Taided discovered that she was more interested in planning a menu for her next dinner party than she was in what she was studying in school. She read every cookbook that she could and tested many recipes on her well-fed friends. She continued her training with several high-end New York City caterers, as well as at Pearl Oyster Bar and the MoMA

Cafés. She is committed to fresh, local, seasonal cuisine, and works in New York City as a private chef.

DANTE BOCCUZZI

Michelin Star chef Dante Boccuzzi returned to his Cleveland, Ohio, roots to open his flagship location, Dante, in the historic Tremont neighborhood. Driven by innovation, Chef Boccuzzi developed a menu of modern American cuisine fused with his traditional Italian background. His second restaurant, Ginko, features modern Japanese sushi and shabu-shabu.

DANIEL BOULUD

Daniel Boulud, a native of Lyon, France, is considered one of America's leading culinary authorities. In New York City, the chef offers Bar Boulud, Café Boulud, db Bistro Moderne, DBGB Kitchen and Bar, Boulud Sud, and Épicerie Boulud, in addition to DANIEL, the renowned Michelin Three-Star Relais & Châteaux member. You'll also find his uniquely ingredients-driven seasonal French–American cooking in Miami and Palm Beach, Florida, and internationally in London, Singapore, and Beijing. Chef Boulud is the recipient of three James Beard Foundation awards, including Outstanding Chef and Outstanding Restaurateur, and was named a Chevalier de la Légion d'Honneur by the French government, as well as Chef of the Year 2011 by the Culinary Institute of America. He is the author of six cookbooks, and the creator and host of the television series *After Hours with Daniel*. The chef has served on the board of directors of Citymeals-on-Wheels since 2000.

SCOTT BOVA

Scott Bova attended the Culinary Institute of America. Upon graduation he joined the team at the Left Bank in Duck, North Carolina (AAA *Four Diamond*). After the Left Bank, he moved to Virginia to work at the Inn at Little Washington (AAA Five Star, *Five Diamond*, Relais & Châteaux). Upon leaving the Inn, Chef Bova was asked to take over as the executive chef at La Fleur Restaurant, which was also awarded a AAA Four Diamond rating under his guidance when he was just twenty-four years old. Working with the same company, Chef Bova took over as corporate executive chef at Food Is Good, Inc., and as a culinary instructor at Jamestown Community College. He then became the corporate executive chef at the Historic Chautauqua Institution, where he oversaw private catering at the President's Cottage. Chef Bova is a private chef and consultant.

JIMMY BRADLEY

Jimmy Bradley is chef–owner of two popular New York City restaurants, the Red Cat and the Harrison, which have become destinations for locals and visitors alike. He has helped diners discover the intrinsic value of classic Mediterranean cuisine, while reinterpreting it for a modern American clientele. He and his recipes are regularly featured in the *New York Times*, *Food & Wine*, *Bon Appétit*, and other food publications, as well as on local and national television programs. He also published *The Red Cat Cookbook*.

ZACHARY BRUELL

More than twenty-five years ago, *Cleveland Magazine* credited chef and restaurateur Zachary Bruell with introducing the area to an emerging West Coast trend of bistro dining and fusion cuisine. Today, he is the only chef in Cleveland, Ohio, to have four successful restaurants within the city limits. In 2004, Chef Bruell opened his signature restaurant, Parallax, in Cleveland's Tremont neighborhood, focusing on fusion seafood and featuring a sushi bar. Two years later, Cleveland Clinic CEO Toby Cosgrove asked Bruell to take over the main restaurant at the InterContinental Cleveland. Chef Bruell created Table 45—an award-winning world-cuisine concept. In 2009, he opened L'Albatros on the campus of Case Western Reserve University. His most recent restaurant concept, Chinato, opened in 2010. Set in Cleveland's East Fourth Street neighborhood, Chinato features a simple yet modern Italian menu.

CRISTINA CASTAÑEDA

Cristina Castañeda arrived in New York City in 1987 as a design student from Guadalajara, Mexico. She landed her first job as a hostess in a popular, twenty-five-year-old Tex-Mex restaurant that eventually became the site of her first restaurant, Café Frida, one of the most respected Mexican restaurants in New York City.

From 1987 to 1998, she continued her studies in design, and then worked in marketing and retail management, all the while keeping restaurant jobs on the side. Cristina now owns four groundbreaking restaurants: Café Frida, Café Ronda, La Rural Bistro, and Rigoletto Pizza. In 2005, she founded Beyond Restaurants Group to operate and manage the restaurant and catering business, in addition to keeping involved in global activities, such as sponsoring cultural events, volunteering time for nonprofit community programs, and participating in fund-raising events.

AMANDA COHEN

Amanda Cohen graduated from the Natural Gourmet Cookery School's Chef's Training Program in 1998, and went on to do everything from interning in the pastry kitchen of Bobby Flay's Mesa Grill to working as a baker in the production kitchen of Blanche's Organic Cafe. After working at DinerBar, an East Harlem diner, for three years, she became the inaugural cook at TeaNY, Moby's Lower East Side vegan teahouse, and then became the executive sous chef at raw-food restaurant Pure Food and Wine. She opened her award-winning, nine-table vegetarian restaurant, Dirt Candy, in the East Village in 2008, and has gone on to win awards from *Gourmet* magazine and the *Village Voice*, among others.

HAROLD DIETERLE

Harold Dieterle's strong Italian-American upbringing (he was raised on Long Island and his mother's Sicilian cooking) is what first inspired him to be a chef. In 1995, he worked his way through some of the top kitchens in Spain. Upon his return, he attended the Culinary Institute of America.

Postgraduation, Harold launched Della Femina's Manhattan restaurant and then moved on to become a chef at Red Bar on Manhattan's Upper East Side. Following Red Bar, Harold took a position at 1770 House, awarded two stars by the *New York Times*. After he met Jimmy Bradley in 2002, his search for just the right restaurant ended. Harold refined his skills in the kitchen at the Harrison under the tutelage of chefs Joey Campanaro and Brian Bistrong. In early 2004, Harold went on sabbatical to Thailand, where he studied with some of that country's top chefs, and learned how to cook best with rare and exotic ingredients. He returned to New York City ready, and opened a place of his own, called Perilla, in the West Village in 2007, followed by his second venture, Kin Shop, in 2010. Harold was the first-season winner of Bravo's *Top Chef*.

PETER ECO

Raised by his grandparents in New York City's Little Italy, Peter Eco was strongly influenced by their cooking techniques developed in Rome and Piacenza. At an early age, he discovered the art of Italian cooking, using the freshest products, cooking them simply and maximizing the tastes and textures as only Italians can do. Since then, numerous great and talented chefs have influenced his cooking styles and recipes, which emphasize French,

Asian, Mediterranean, Moroccan, and American fine dining.

Chef Eco's passion for food and wine exploded while he attended Johnson & Wales University in Providence, Rhode Island. After graduating in 1986, he returned to New York City, and began his professional career at Buds under the direction of Chef Jonathan Waxman. He has since worked in restaurants all over the Northeast, and in 2008 he was hired to open Chef Tom Colicchio's AAA Four Diamond Award–winning Craftsteak at Foxwoods Resort & Casino. He is based in Massachusetts.

BRAD FARMERIE

Brad Farmerie's culinary passion comes from training in some of Europe's top kitchens and eating in markets, dining halls, and myriad eateries all over the world. An *Iron Chef America* winner and recipient of numerous awards, including Food Arts' Emerging Tastemaker and *Global Magazine*'s Top 50 Chefs to Watch, Chef Farmerie's inimitable style has earned his restaurants substantial critical acclaim, including a Michelin Star for PUBLIC for three consecutive years.

JAY FOSTER

Chef–owner Jay Foster, formerly of Emmy's Spaghetti Shack and Bluejay Café, is the creative force behind farmerbrown's unique take on soul food, along with his partner, Deanna Sison. The restaurant's goal is to provide the freshest possible organic ingredients for its wholesome southern classics and present them lovingly to their local communities in a down-home, soulful atmosphere. From the entrées to the cocktails to the interior design, everything is handmade and carefully crafted by the staff. In addition, farmerbrown is all about supporting local and African-American farmers, using organic, biodynamic, and/or sustainably raised foods and beverages, whenever possible.

LEIGH FRIEND

Leigh Friend has a passion for local and seasonal ingredients. After attending New England Culinary Institute in Burlington, Vermont, she decided that pastry was her true calling. She has baked artisan breads in Boston, made wedding cakes in California, and created gourmet craft services in New York City for the film and commercial industry. She is the pastry chef for Elsewhere and Casellula in New York City.

TERRY FRISHMAN

Terry Frishman is a culinary dream maker who loves brainstorming, marketing, and taking food businesses to the next level. She consults for food entrepreneurs, start-ups, and established businesses, including Sarabeth's Kitchen, for which she is international sales manager. Terry teaches at three New York City culinary schools, where she offers the courses "How to Launch & Market Food Products" and "Write Great Business Plans," as well as "What I Wish I Knew Before Starting My Food Business." She also runs an inspiring, action-oriented Next Level Workshop series. Vice president of the New York Women's Culinary Alliance, Terry was formerly president of the Roundtable for Women in Food Service, and she is on the board of the International Wine & Food Society. She has an MBA from Columbia University, and won many awards while working at Kraft General Foods and *Newsweek International,* before starting her consultancy, Creative Marketing Workshops, in New York City.

PETER GIANNAKAS

Peter Giannakas, microbiologist turned chef–owner of Ovelia Psistaria Bar, takes his experimental background and brings it into the kitchen. Building around traditional Greek fare, his dishes transform into contemporary delights that become new classics. Without any formal training, most of what he has learned comes from his lifelong apprenticeship with his mother's cooking at home and his father's thirty-five-year career as a chef. The inspiration for most of his dishes peek out of the cupboards of his childhood, where traditional Greek products such as Greek coffee, candied figs, and ouzo are used in unconventional ways, paired with meats and pastas, adding a new dimension to Greek cuisine.

DOMINIC GIULIANO

Born and raised in Newport Beach, California, Dominic Giuliano graduated from the Culinary Institute of America in 1995. He landed his first job out of culinary school at the Ritz Carlton in Laguna Niguel, California. Opening restaurants, creating menus, and building a strong back-of-the-house team are among his specialties. He has opened more than twenty-five restaurants since 1995. Most notably in New York City, he opened PS450, the Volstead, Punch & Judy, and Suba. In 2009, he was awarded Best Crab Cake at the annual New Jersey Crab Cake Festival. He is the executive chef and co-owner of Choza Taqueria in New York City.

COLLEEN GRAPES

A New Jersey native, Colleen was first introduced to baking by her grandmother and great-grandmother, who, during the holidays, filled their apartment with freshly baked cookies. Colleen attended Johnson & Wales University, studying food-service management and pastry arts. During school, she worked at Providence's Al Forno with chefs George Germon and Johanne Killeen, and after graduation she moved to New York City, where she worked at Aja as assistant pastry chef under Gary Robbins. Following a six-month sabbatical in Europe, Colleen moved to Boston, where she was named executive pastry chef of Café Louis. From there, she went to the Hamptons to work at the Art of Eating Catering. She then moved back to the city, and enjoyed working in some of the city's top restaurants, including Rue 57, the Sea Grill, and Dressler's. She is now pastry chef at both the Red Cat, where she works with Jimmy Bradley and Bill McDaniel, and the Harrison.

RICHARD HETZLER

Richard Hetzler is Restaurant Associates' (RA) executive chef at the Mitsitam Native Foods Café at the National Museum of the American Indian. After graduating from Baltimore International Culinary College, he honed his skills in fine-dining restaurants and hotels, including Elkridge Furnace Inn, Jefferson Hotel, Maryland Inn, and Treaty of Paris Restaurant.

In 1998, Chef Hetzler was asked to join RA as the executive chef at the National Museum of Natural History (NMNH). During his time at NMNH, he helped create five new RA food venues. He was also part of the catering service team for RA's parent company, the Compass Group, at the 2002 Winter Olympics in Salt Lake City, Utah. Chef Hetzler was approached to head the Mitsitam Native Foods Café at the earliest stages of menu planning. He spearheaded the research and tasting process that resulted in the five unique regional menus and a truly one-of-a-kind dining experience that reflects and complements the museum's mission to educate visitors about native cultures. He also created and published the award-winning *Mitsitam Café Cookbook*.

DANA JACOBI

Blogging at www.danasmarketbasket.com, Dana Jacobi focuses on seasonal produce, ethnic cooking, cookbook reviews, and sharing recipes. Her latest book, *Cook & Freeze*, shows how to preserve the best and have delicious meals ready to serve anytime. Also the author of *12 Best Foods Cookbook*, Dana lives in New York City.

NICOLE KAPLAN

Raised in Spring Valley, New York, Nicole Kaplan spent years as a professional flute player, performing all over the globe. Between performances, she spent her time researching and feasting in the great historic culinary centers of Europe. Upon returning to New York, Nicole enrolled in Peter Kump's New York Cooking School, where she graduated with a Blue Ribbon in 1997. She quickly landed a job as pastry assistant at Sign of the Dove, then went on to work at Osteria del Circo and then Eleven Madison Park, where she developed a signature dessert menu for the restaurant, collaborating closely with Executive Chef Daniel Humm. Nicole then became executive pastry chef at Del Posto, where she worked in collaboration with Mario Batali and Lidia Bastianich.

Nicole's desserts have received numerous accolades and awards. She was included in *New York Magazine*'s Top 10 Rising Star Pastry Chefs in 2003, and was also named one of the Top 10 Pastry Chefs. She has served as a consultant to Shake Shack and Hudson Yards Catering. Nicole is currently on the faculty at the Institute of Culinary Education.

DOUGLAS KATZ

Douglas Katz is the owner and executive chef of Fire Food and Drink, located at historic Shaker Square in Cleveland, Ohio. For the past decade, Chef Katz has supported local farmers and food artisans, and is an international advocate for a food system that is sustainable, healthful, and local. He also serves as a celebrity chef ambassador for the Monterey Bay Aquarium's Cooking for Solutions program, which promotes environmentally responsible fishing and fish farming.

In 1998, *Esquire* magazine honored Fire as one of America's best new restaurants, and in 1999, Chef Katz received the *Reader's Digest* Rising Star of American Cuisine Award. Fire also received Best Restaurant Awards in 2005 from both *Cleveland* and *Northern Ohio Live* magazines. He was recognized in Crain's Cleveland Business "Who's Who: 150 Names to Know in Northeast Ohio" in 2010. He is a graduate of the Culinary Institute of America, and holds a BS from the University of Denver School of Hotel and Restaurant Management. His restaurant's mission statement is "Simple food, sustainable practices, igniting the community."

SETH KOSLOW

Seth Koslow is a budding, self-taught amateur chef who was featured on the Food Network's *Grill It! with Bobby Flay*. Seth prides himself on making dishes that anybody can replicate, with little or no training. He likes to keep his creations simple, colorful, and delicious, without too much fanfare. Seth also likes to re-create the dishes he eats at local restaurants, imparting his own spin on foods he already enjoys. As a student, Seth founded a side project called Koslow's Kitchen, which provides barbecue cooking services for private parties.

JAMES LAIRD

Upon graduation from the Culinary Institute of America, Chef James Laird traveled to Europe to hone his skills under the tutelage of renowned chefs Georges Blanc and Alain Pic. During the early '90s, he held positions at Lespinasse, the River Café, and Aureole, eventually moving on to New Jersey's esteemed Ryland Inn. During his tenure as sous chef, the restaurant received an "Extraordinary" rating from the *New York Times* (the equivalent of four stars). He opened Restaurant Serenade with his wife, Nancy Sheridan Laird, to great critical praise in 1996. Today, Chef Laird is one of the most acclaimed chefs in New Jersey. The *New York Times* named him "one of the best classically trained chefs in New Jersey," and *New Jersey Monthly* has consistently rated Restaurant Serenade among "the best of the best." Chef Laird—a yoga and golf devotee—also raises organic, heirloom vegetables in a raised-bed garden, as well as heirloom chickens.

JACKIE M. LEE

Jackie Lee is a private chef working for an exclusive family in Manhattan, New York. She has been a chef for more than seventeen years, with diverse culinary appointments. Jackie has worked and traveled around the world aboard some of the most prestigious megayachts. She has also made many television appearances, most notably as the winner of the Food Network's hit show *Chopped*. Jackie is also a featured expert on www.genconnect.com. She is writing a book due out in 2012.

EVE LINDENBLATT NASETTI

Eve Lindenblatt-Nasetti, graduate of L'Academie de Cuisine, founded Extra Hands and Eve's Apple, where her delectable recipes have graced palates from New York to California. Eve specializes in custom menu planning for private parties from her current home base in south Florida.

MARC MATYAS

Marc Matyas has owned and operated Nolita House, a successful New York City restaurant and catering company in downtown Manhattan, since 2004. A self-taught restaurateur, Marc has worked in virtually every position within the restaurant and catering world, including general manager and executive chef. Upon graduating Columbia University in 1996 with an honors degree, Marc worked in hospitality for a while, then worked for the New York State government before successfully launching two software companies.

Marc transitioned back into hospitality by opening Nolita House, and he has grown his dream into a successful restaurant and catering brand that has garnered much industry kudos, including *New York Magazine*'s Best Brunch with Music and Best Comfort Food recognition from CitySearch. Marc lives in Manhattan with his son, Maddox; his two pugs, Frank and Penelope; and his loving and patient wife, Kailah.

LESLIE MEENAN

Leslie Meenan is co-owner with brother Sean Meenan (founder) of Café Habana. She has been involved with the restaurants since 1999, handling both creative development and assisting in management of each location.

Leslie is a native New Yorker who grew up on the Upper East Side of Manhattan and has also lived throughout the New York City area, including in Brooklyn near the company's second location, Habana Outpost. She is passionate about environmental causes and promoting a green lifestyle. She is an investor and contributing travel writer for *Positively Green* magazine, a national environmental magazine geared toward women.

LAURIE JON MORAN

Originally from Northamptonshire, England, Laurie Jon Moran graduated from the culinary program at Northampton College, and then began his career at the Michelin Two Star Le Manoir aux Quat'Saisons in Oxfordshire, England. During his time there, Le Manoir hosted a number of top American chefs, which led to Laurie's receiving an invitation to work at DANIEL in New York. While at DANIEL, Laurie achieved the rank of pastry sous chef, and was part of the team that earned the restaurant's third Michelin Star. Laurie then became executive pastry chef at Terrance Brennan's Michelin Two Star restaurant, Picholine, before moving on to work as pastry sous chef at Thomas Keller's Per Se.

PICHET ONG

As a self-taught chef, Pichet Ong has worked with culinary luminaries, including Jean-Georges Vongerichten and Max Brenner. Pichet has been named one of the Top Ten Pastry Chefs in America by *Pastry Arts & Design* and *Chocolatier*, and was selected as a "Pastry Provocateur" by *Food & Wine*. In 2002, he was named Starchefs.com's "Rising Star" and featured in the prestigious "The Chef" column of the *New York Times* for four weeks. His desserts, including those from Spice Market, RM, and 66, have garnered numerous "Best of" awards. He is a multiple nominee for the James Beard Award in several national categories. His work frequently appears in *Bon Appétit*, *Food Arts*, the *New Yorker*, *Elle*, *New York Magazine*, *Time Out*, *People*, *Vogue*, *Condé Nast Traveler*, *Out*, *Harper's Bazaar*, W, and *O, The Oprah Magazine*. He has been on *Iron Chef America*, *Martha Stewart Live*, *CBS News*, *Emeril's Live*, and *LX.TV*.

Pichet lives in New York, and consults on culinary projects worldwide, including the recently opened Coppelia and Qi in New York City. He is working on a blog about food, music, and love in New York, and opening Batch Bakery. He has written two cookbooks, *The Sweet Spot* and *Desserts on a Whim*.

NAOMI POMEROY

Naomi and her sous chef, Mika Paredes, first welcomed customers into Beast on September 27, 2007. Accolades and awards have followed: She was featured in *Gourmet* and *Elle* magazines; *Bon Appétit* named Naomi as one of the top six of a new generation of female chefs in September 2008; and *Food & Wine* recognized her as one of the 10 Best New Chefs in America for 2009. Locally, Naomi was voted Chef of the Year for 2008 by *Portland Monthly*; and Beast was honored as Restaurant of the Year for 2008 by the *Oregonian*, and chosen as Best Brunch by the *Willamette Weekly*. In 2009, Naomi bought out her partners to become the sole owner of Beast. In March 2010, she was selected as a finalist for the prestigious James Beard awards in the category of Best Chef Pacific Northwest. In October 2010, *Marie Claire* magazine named Naomi one of the eighteen most powerful women in business. In April 2011, she appeared as a contestant on the third season of Bravo's *Top Chef Masters*.

BRIAN PRESTON-CAMPBELL

Brian Preston-Campbell is a professional food stylist and former chef. A graduate of the Culinary Institute of America, he has brought his talent for food styling to national ad campaigns for such companies as Starbucks, Absolut, Nestlé, Godiva, and Smucker's. His creative food styling has also appeared in magazines such as *O, The Oprah Magazine*, the *New York Times Magazine, Prevention*, and *Men's Health*. In addition, he was the food stylist for several books, including *The Sneaky Chef* and *Good Spirits*, winner of an IACP Cookbook Award for Food Photography and Styling. He lives in New York with his wife and two children.

CLAUDIA RODEN

Claudia Roden was born and brought up in Cairo, and educated in Paris and London, where she lives. Widely admired as both a great cook and a fine writer, she is the author of several books, including *The New Book of Middle Eastern Food* and *The Book of Jewish Food. The Food of Italy* grew out of "The Taste of Italy," a series of articles she wrote for the *Sunday Times* of London. Her writing has been awarded many prestigious international prizes, including five Glenfiddich Awards, the James Beard Award in the United States, and the Versailles Award in France.

SANDRO ROMANO

Growing up in Switzerland with parents of Italian descent, Sandro Romano knew he wanted to be a chef by age thirteen. He apprenticed in Switzerland's prestigious Le Relais restaurant, and then began to work at Beau Rivage Palace and as a private chef in La Chaux-de-Fonds. In 1996, Romano attended the acclaimed École des Cafetier et Hôtelier. He worked as Chef de Cuisine at Restaurant La Bohème in Neuchâtel, Switzerland, for two years, and then spent four years working as executive sous chef with Chef Michael Romano and renowned restaurateur Danny Meyer at Union Square Café in New York City. Romano met famed chef Rocco DiSpirito, who brought him on to consult for restaurateur Jeffrey Chodorow at Tuscan Steak. The restaurant soon emerged as Tuscan, and Romano became executive chef. In 2003/2004, Romano had a chance to join Danny Meyer's Eleven Madison Park as chef de cuisine just prior to opening the Modern in the MoMA in 2005, as chef de cuisine.

GABRIEL RUCKER

Food & Wine magazine named Chef Rucker one of the country's Best New Chefs in 2007. In 2008, 2009, 2010, and 2011, he was nominated for the James Beard Foundation's Rising Star Chef. In 2011, he won.

Instead of a formal culinary education, Chef Rucker opted for a hands-on approach. After leaving his native California for Oregon in 2003, he landed a job at the highly regarded Paley's Place in Portland, and eventually moved on to become the sous chef at the Gotham Building Tavern. In June 2006, he started at Le Pigeon with rustic French-Spanish-Californian-Oregonian-style fare. He was mentioned on *Food & Wine*'s Best New Chefs of 2007 list, *Portland Monthly* named him Chef of the Year, and the *Oregonian* dubbed him Rising Star Chef of 2007. *Restaurant Hospitality* magazine also named him Rising Star Chef of 2007. In December 2010, Gabriel's second restaurant, Little Bird, opened to critical acclaim.

JONATHON SAWYER

Cleveland native Chef Jonathon Sawyer learned to cook when he was thirteen. After graduating from the Pennsylvania Institute of Culinary Arts, Sawyer went on to work at the Biltmore Hotel in Miami. One year later, he was working alongside renowned chef Charlie Palmer in New York City at Kitchen 22. Sawyer then worked with Michael Symon to open Lolita back in his hometown of Cleveland, and Parea in New York City. After receiving a two-star review from the *New York Times* and a five-star review from *Time Out New York* for his work at Parea, Sawyer moved back to Cleveland to pursue his dream of opening his own restaurant.

In 2007, Chef Sawyer became the chef–partner of Bar Cento, a modern Roman *enoteca* in Ohio City. His work received many accolades, including *Restaurant Hospitality* & *Gayot*'s Rising Star Chef and *Northern Ohio Live*'s Best New Restaurant. In 2008, Sawyer opened the Greenhouse Tavern, inspired by his commitment to use local, sustainable ingredients and environmentally conscious building materials. Sawyer also collaborated with the Green Restaurant Association to become the first certified green restaurant in the state of Ohio. In July 2011, Chef Sawyer opened his second certified green restaurant, Noodlecat, an American Japanese mash-up. The Greenhouse Tavern was named one of the top ten best new restaurants in the United States by *Bon Appétit*, and Chef Sawyer was also honored as one of *Food & Wine*'s Best New Chefs in 2011. He has appeared on the Food Network's *Dinner Impossible* and *Iron Chef America*.

DAN SILVERMAN

As the executive chef of the Standard Grill in New York's Standard Hotel, acclaimed Chef Dan Silverman utilizes the freshest market ingredients and a wide array of local purveyors to create refined versions of classic American dishes. A graduate of the French Culinary institute, Silverman started his career at Bouley, where he became sous chef, and at Alison on Dominick Street, where he earned *Food & Wine's* "Best New Chef" award, as its executive chef. Silverman later worked as executive chef at Danny Meyer's Union Square Café, helping the restaurant maintain its coveted *Zagat Guide* number-one most popular restaurant position during his four-year tenure. In 2003, he was given the opportunity to open Lever House, which was nominated as a Best New Restaurant by the James Beard Foundation the following year. Silverman authored a book, *The Lever House Cookbook*. His menu at the Standard Grill is rooted in the traditional American chophouse, offering inspired updates of timeless dishes and a focus on the grill. Since the restaurant's opening in 2009, it has earned critical acclaim.

ALLEN STAFFORD

Allen Stafford has been hosting parties, producing shows and events, and making it happen since high school. He has also worked in the film, theater, accounting, and psychiatric industries, among many others. Allen is a vital part of the creation of Casellula, New York's premier cheese-and-wine café. He designed the original pastry menu, and also created the café's artwork. On Casellula's east wall hangs *Farm Glory*, his assemblage of foil capsules from wine bottles affixed to a wood panel with copper carpet tacks. Allen also supervised the interior design of Casellula's sister restaurant, Elsewhere, where he will gladly make a reservation for you and greet you with his soft southern smile.

MARTHA STEWART

Martha Stewart is the author of many best-selling books on food, entertaining, gardening, and home renovation. She is chairman and chief executive officer of Martha Stewart Living Omnimedia. She lives in Connecticut and on Long Island.

HONG THAIMEE

Born and raised in Chiang Mai, Thailand, Ngamprom "Hong" Thaimee is a former model and television personality who followed her passion for food all the way to New York. Trained in the art of authentic Thai cuisine by M. L. Sirichalerm Savsti (McDang), Thailand's most celebrated chef, Hong has worked in some of New York City's best restaurants, including Kittichai, Spice Market, and Perry St. She has also worked in the kitchens of the five-star Mandarin Oriental Dhara Devi Hotel in her hometown.

Hong performed cooking demonstrations on behalf of the Thai Trade Center and Thai Tourism Authority, and was the executive chef of Maze Café, a hip local eatery in Chiang Mai. Additionally, she catered private affairs for distinguished guests around the globe, including fashion celebrities and members of the Thai and Indian royal families. She considers herself an ambassador of Thai cuisine, and her goal is to share the best of her country's culinary culture with the world.

GUILLAUME THIVET

Born in Béziers in the south of France, where his family owned a restaurant on the beach, Chef Guillaume Thivet received his culinary degree from the Culinary Institute of Montpellier. Traveling broadened his experience with different cuisines, from the Relais & Châteaux Hôtel Le Toiny in St. Barts, to Michelin One-Star La Côte Bleue in Bouzigues in the south of France, to the famed Ryland Inn in New Jersey, where he met his mentor, Chef Craig Shelton. Taking the opportunity to work in New York City, Chef Thivet joined the opening team at Dennis Foy's eponymous restaurant, then Mercat, Bouley, and later Bouley Market. He is now the executive chef of Cadaqués, a modern Catalan tapas bar and restaurant in the Williamsburg neighborhood of Brooklyn.

PETER VAUTHY

Executive chef Peter Vauthy grew up in New Jersey, watching his great-grandmother create such Italian dishes as zeppoli. His cooking is inspired by family classics but includes his own unique perspective, marrying tradition and innovation.

In addition to numerous guest-chef appearances with the James Beard Foundation, Chef Vauthy was named Innovator of the Year by the National Beef Association, and was instrumental in *Playboy* magazine naming Red, The Steakhouse, one of the Top 10 Steakhouses in America in 2007.

JEAN-GEORGES VONGERICHTEN

Jean-Georges Vongerichten is one of the world's most famous chefs, responsible for the operation and success of a constellation of three- and four-star restaurants in the United States, United Kingdom, and Shanghai. He has published numerous cookbooks, including *Simple Cuisine*; *Cooking at Home with a Four-Star Chef*, for which he won the Best Cookbook Award from the James Beard Foundation in 1999; and *Simple to Spectacular*. In October 2007, he released *Asian Flavors of Jean-Georges*, featuring beloved recipes from his restaurants Spice Market and Vong.

Jean-Georges is the chef in residence for *CITY* magazine, and master cook for *Food & Wine* magazine. He has appeared on *Live! with Regis and Kelly*, the *Today* show, *Good Morning America*, *Martha Stewart Living*, *Everyday Elegance with Colin Cowie*, *The Early Show* on CBS, and TV Food Network, and in the 1995 PBS series *In Julia's Kitchen with Master Chefs*.

BOB WAGGONER

Bob Waggoner grew up in Southern California, and began in the kitchen of Michael Roberts at Trumps in West Hollywood, and then went to work for a succession of great chefs in the Burgundy region of France. His first position as chef was at Members, a private club in Caracas, Venezuela, at age twenty-three. He returned to France, where he met his wife, and became the first American to own a restaurant in France, the much acclaimed Monte Cristo. Eleven years later, Bob returned to the States, and joined the Wild Boar in Nashville, earning the restaurant the coveted AAA Five Diamond Award, as well as the Grand Award from *Wine Spectator*. The rich, multicultural cuisine of the French Low Country drew him to South Carolina, where he helmed the elegant Charleston Grill at Charleston Place for twelve years, and was nominated by the James Beard Foundation as Best Chef in the Southeast.

Chef Waggoner is one of the few Americans to be knighted as a Chevalier with the Ordre du Mérite Agricole, and he is the only American to have worked with Gérard Boyer, Pierre Gagnaire, and Marc Meneau, three of the French honorees with whom he was acknowledged at *Gourmet* magazine's event France's 10 Greatest Chefs. He has appeared on CNN, the Travel Channel, and CBS's *The Early Show,* and has also earned an Emmy for his television show *Off the Menu* with Turner South. He now has his own PBS program, *UCook! with Chef Bob*.

ABOUT THE DOUGY CENTER

The Dougy Center was founded in 1982 by Beverly Chappell, in tribute to Dougy Turno, a young boy who died of an inoperable brain tumor at age thirteen. Before meeting Dougy, Bev was a registered nurse who had worked in the area of death and dying since 1974. Through her work, she found most people were uncomfortable when faced with death and grief, and that doctors, clergy, hospital staff, and school personnel often did not have the training to support children in their grief. This reality inspired Bev to attend the first of many seminars and lectures by Dr. Elisabeth Kübler-Ross, pioneer and author in the field of death and dying.

In August 1981, Dougy wrote a poignant letter to Dr. Kübler-Ross, asking why no one would speak to him of dying, even when he was facing his own death. Dr. Kübler-Ross corresponded with Dougy, and encouraged Beverly Chappell to meet him and his family when they visited Oregon Health Sciences University for experimental treatment. Bev clearly saw in Dougy a thirst for life and a deep compassion for others that many never attain, even in their older years. After Dougy's death later that year, his wisdom and inspiration stayed with Bev, and led her to start support groups for grieving children. Those first families in need of grief support met in Bev's basement family room in her southeast Portland home. Soon, a board of directors was recruited, volunteer facilitators were trained, and The Dougy Center entered a phenomenal period of growth.

Today, The Dougy Center serves four hundred children and their 250 adult family members each month. Its twenty-six open-ended peer support groups meet every other week, and are divided by age, type of death (illness, sudden death, murder, suicide), and who died (parent, sibling). The concurrent twenty-six adult support groups meet at the same time for the caregiver of the child or teen who is attending the group. Since its founding, The Dougy Center has served more than thirty thousand children, teens, and their families, and has received national and international acclaim for its pioneering peer support model for helping children cope with the deaths of family members. Through its National Training Program and training materials, thousands have learned how to help grieving children, and five hundred programs modeled after The Dougy Center have been established worldwide.

The Dougy Center relies on the generosity of individuals, businesses, and foundations. It receives no government funding, and is supported entirely by private donations and professional training fees. It never charges families for its services.

To find out more about peer support groups at The Dougy Center (www.dougy.org), and how you can help, you may call 503.775.5683 or e-mail help@dougy.org.

ACKNOWLEDGMENTS

The ability we each have to create anything and everything we want is uncanny. We can essentially put our dreams in motion because of other people. It took one idea, and one person to believe in that idea, and one person to share that idea, and the next thing I knew, the *I Love Corn* cookbook was born!

I printed three hundred copies of the first version of this book in 2007, and it would absolutely *not* have been possible without the following *extraordinary* people: graphic designer Shir Konas of Perceive Creative (NYC), food photographer Bill Brady, Chef Dominic Giuliano, food stylist Brian Preston-Campbell, über-talented writers Jean Tang and Peg San Felippo, and my best friend on the planet, Elijah Selby. I cannot thank you all enough for bringing this vision to life.

Thank you to all of the people who made the summer 2007 soft-launch party possible. Whether you donated auction items, venue space, food, or frequent-flyer miles, or worked the door, passed hors d'oeuvres, or simply showed up, it was a night to remember!

Thanks to Jayne who introduced me to Andrews McMeel Publishing, where Kirsty Melville and Jean Lucas guided me through the occasionally daunting process of writing my first book. Thank you to all of the chefs and to the PR companies representing the chefs who donated delicious recipes to this great cause. Thank you to everyone who helped me test and retest recipes. With your amazingly detailed feedback, we were able to make this cookbook super user friendly for amateur chefs (a.k.a. home cooks) like me!

A huge *thank-you* to all of my fellow BNI members in Lucky 62, and to many of your friends and family, who helped me make contacts to grow the recipe list and test corn recipes all summer long. I hope you had as much fun and learned as much as I did along the way!

A special thank-you to Rubina Costabile, Rian Moore, Brennan Wood, Myra Goldstein Orenstein, Danny Orenstein, Eve Lindenblatt Nasetti, Alex Constantopes, the Chansidines, Amy Young, Dustin Lara, and Nathan Seven Scott.

And finally, a big bundle of love and gratitude goes to my brother, Brian, who is a trained chef and took my late-night calls when I was testing recipes; to my mother, Joyce, who inspires me to be the eternal optimist I am; and to Anthony, who supports me in all that I am and all that I do.

METRIC CONVERSIONS AND EQUIVALENTS

METRIC CONVERSION FORMULAS

To Convert	Multiply
Ounces to grams	Ounces by 28.35
Pounds to kilograms	Pounds by 0.454
Teaspoons to milliliters	Teaspoons by 4.93
Tablespoons to milliliters	Tablespoons by 14.79
Fluid ounces to milliliters	Fluid ounces by 29.57
Cups to milliliters	Cups by 236.59
Cups to liters	Cups by 0.236
Pints to liters	Pints by 0.473
Quarts to liters	Quarts by 0.946
Gallons to liters	Gallons by 3.785
Inches to centimeters	Inches by 2.54

APPROXIMATE METRIC EQUIVALENTS

Volume

¼ teaspoon	1 milliliter
½ teaspoon	2.5 milliliters
¾ teaspoon	4 milliliters
1 teaspoon	5 milliliters
1¼ teaspoons	6 milliliters
1½ teaspoons	7.5 milliliters
1¾ teaspoons	8.5 milliliters
2 teaspoons	10 milliliters
1 tablespoon (½ fluid ounce)	15 milliliters
2 tablespoons (1 fluid ounce)	30 milliliters
¼ cup	60 milliliters
⅓ cup	80 milliliters
½ cup (4 fluid ounces)	120 milliliters
⅔ cup	160 milliliters
¾ cup	180 milliliters
1 cup (8 fluid ounces)	240 milliliters
1¼ cups	300 milliliters
1½ cups (12 fluid ounces)	360 milliliters
1⅔ cups	400 milliliters
2 cups (1 pint)	460 milliliters
3 cups	700 milliliters
4 cups (1 quart)	0.95 liter
1 quart plus ¼ cup	1 liter
4 quarts (1 gallon)	3.8 liters

Weight

¼ ounce	7 grams
½ ounce	14 grams
¾ ounce	21 grams
1 ounce	28 grams
1¼ ounces	35 grams
1½ ounces	42.5 grams
1⅔ ounces	45 grams
2 ounces	57 grams
3 ounces	85 grams
4 ounces (¼ pound)	113 grams
5 ounces	142 grams
6 ounces	170 grams
7 ounces	198 grams
8 ounces (½ pound)	227 grams
16 ounces (1 pound)	454 grams
35¼ ounces (2.2 pounds)	1 kilogram

Length

⅛ inch	3 millimeters
¼ inch	6 millimeters
½ inch	1.25 centimeters
1 inch	2.5 centimeters
2 inches	5 centimeters
2½ inches	6 centimeters
4 inches	10 centimeters
5 inches	13 centimeters
6 inches	15.25 centimeters
12 inches (1 foot)	30 centimeters

OVEN TEMPERATURES

To convert Fahrenheit to Celsius, subtract 32 from Fahrenheit, multiply the result by 5, then divide by 9.

Description	Fahrenheit	Celsius	British Gas Mark
Very cool	200°	95°	0
Very cool	225°	110°	¼
Very cool	250°	120°	½
Cool	275°	135°	1
Cool	300°	150°	2
Warm	325°	165°	3
Moderate	350°	175°	4
Moderately hot	375°	190°	5
Fairly hot	400°	200°	6
Hot	425°	220°	7
Very hot	450°	230°	8
Very hot	475°	245°	9

COMMON INGREDIENTS AND THEIR APPROXIMATE EQUIVALENTS

1 cup uncooked rice = 225 grams

1 cup all-purpose flour = 140 grams

1 stick butter (4 ounces • ½ cup • 8 tablespoons) = 110 grams

1 cup butter (8 ounces • 2 sticks • 16 tablespoons) = 220 grams

1 cup brown sugar, firmly packed = 225 grams

1 cup granulated sugar = 200 grams

Information compiled from a variety of sources, including *Recipes into Type* by Joan Whitman and Dolores Simon (Newton, MA: Biscuit Books, 2000); *The New Food Lover's Companion* by Sharon Tyler Herbst (Hauppauge, NY: Barron's, 1995); and *Rosemary Brown's Big Kitchen Instruction Book* (Kansas City, MO: Andrews McMeel, 1998).

INDEX